Coloring
Outside
Autism's Lines

Coloring
Outside
Autism's Lines

50+ Activities, Adventures, and Celebrations
for Families with Children with Autism

SUSAN WALTON

 sourcebooks

Published by Sourcebooks, Inc.
P.O. Box 4410, Naperville, Illinois 60567-4410
(630) 961-3900
Fax: (630) 961-2168
www.sourcebooks.com

Library of Congress Cataloging-in-Publication Data

Walton, Susan.
    Coloring outside autism's lines: 50+ activities, adventures, and celebrations for families with children with autism / by Susan Walton.
        p. cm.
    1. Autistic children--Family relationships. 2. Parents of autistic children. 3. Family recreation. I. Title.
    RJ506.A9W36 2010
    618.92'85882--dc22
                        2010027320

Printed and bound in the United States of America.
            VP 10 9 8 7 6 5 4 3 2 1

To Timothy, Drew, Jamie, and Katherine.
The funnest family ever.

Contents

· · · · ·

Introduction

Enjoy Life, Even if Autism Is Along for the Ride

* * * * *

Like most women today, I do a lot of things. But mostly, I'm a mom. Various other words have been added to that description over the last ten years: I'm a mom of three. I'm a mom of twins. I've been a working mom and a stay-at-home mom. I can be a kind-of-strict mom and a sometimes-silly mom. I'm a mom who cooks. But perhaps the label that defines me best is that I am the mom of a child with autism.

My son was a little shy of two years old when he was diagnosed with autism. My experience was not much different than that of a lot of other parents I know. My pediatrician missed the signs even though we pointed out concerns. We beat ourselves up for a long time for not getting him diagnosed sooner. And I was in my last month of another pregnancy (twins) when the psychologist said "that word." No matter what my husband and I thought when we stepped into the office that day, we were not ready to hear it.

It changed everything. And I'm sure it changed everything for you too. Even if your child is not on the autism spectrum, if he or she has special needs of another kind, you've entered into that new world where your family falls outside "the norm." There are a zillion things you are supposed to be doing along with everything you already do. And there is never enough time or money to do it all.

We need to change the way we see ourselves, the ways we parent, our immediate future, and our long-term future. But we go on. We put it into some kind of perspective, and we change. And almost immediately, we get busy trying to overcome it. Every family has different experiences and outcomes with therapy or intervention. But every single one of us works hard to procure and provide something therapeutic every single day.

Every child with autism is completely unique, so all of us modify our lives to accommodate the particular variety of autism that affects our family. I know that my child's issues aren't the same as your child's issues. But no matter how different it is for us, we have a lot in common too. One of the biggest things we have in common is how much we worry. We don't know what the future holds for our kids, and there is a lot to worry about.

There are difficult days, exhausting days that sap all of our resources. We spend so much time arranging and performing therapy, finding funding, driving from appointment to appointment, researching, furthering battles with insurance companies, continuing dialogues with caseworkers, and negotiating with school districts. And of course there's everything else that parents do, like grocery shopping, working a job, housecleaning, pediatrician and dentist visits, and so on. But every routine thing is a lot harder than it ought to be, harder than we expected it to be. Even as years go by and things get a bit easier, they will never be as easy as they are for everyone else, not by a long shot.

The impact of all of this is that each day is hard. We're spread too thin. There are days when autism feels like a lifetime punishment for an unknown crime. We look at friends who are arranging playdates, signing up for summer camps, or planning birthday parties with ease and can't help but wonder: Why isn't it that way for me?

I went through a stage when every little boy I saw made my throat tighten. I had to look away from every child I saw in the supermarket because every little boy in the world seemed to remind me of what my son was missing, what I couldn't give him. Instead of running around exploring the world and drinking in life, my little boy was working endlessly and painstakingly to learn concepts that seem to come naturally to everyone else.

But the biggest mistake we can make is to put family fun at a low priority. It is easy to be consumed by the role autism forces us to play. We are caretakers, therapists, nutritionists, nurses, taxi drivers, and so much more. But for the sake of your child and your family, having fun needs to form a central part of any intervention and therapy you pursue.

The best way to increase your child's connectedness and ability to form attachments is to make sure that spending time together is as rewarding as possible. So often when treating autism, the term "reward" is used to describe a tangible or fleeting benefit provided by an adult who is trying to coax a desired behavior. There are styles of therapy built on the premise that controlling rewards leads to desirable behavior. But the feeling of reward that comes from access to a toy or earning a sticker is nothing compared to the feelings of joy and satisfaction associated with having fun with the people who are part of a child's life every day. In order to teach your child that connecting with family is rewarding, you have to *make* it rewarding. It has to feel pleasurable, warm, and gratifying—not momentary and fleeting and immediately followed by another demand.

Pay attention to what your child considers fun and then put as much effort into enjoying a day together as you do into procuring therapy. Because the pursuit of fun is therapy in its own way. And it has outrageous benefits for the rest of the family too. Having a child with autism in the family pushes us to seek out interests that are off the beaten path, to find experiences that especially might work for our spectrum child. Setting out on the popular family fun activities probably won't fulfill us, because they have been generally manufactured to please the most typical kind of family, and we can't be called one of those. We need to modify usual destinations to work for us or sometimes avoid them completely. So we need to get creative, try new things, and take chances. If necessity is the mother of invention, creativity is the maiden aunt of autism. (You may not have to include her in family time, but when you do, it is always more fun!)

Try to enter weekends with an open mind and a sense of adventure. Discover new experiences together and activities that work on some level for everyone. Of course you can continue to enjoy and repeat the tried and true...but try to add one new thing! No matter what you decide to do, if you approach your time together with a sense of fun, it will bring your family closer. Running from appointment to appointment is real work, for you and for your child. It is work for his siblings too, whether they go along to wait or simply miss out on their parents' attention. There have to be times when you turn off the work and relax and enjoy each other's company.

And even if a little voice in the back of your head is saying, "Wow, this might strengthen trunk muscles" or "this encourages language," turn down the volume on your internal therapy voice as low as it can go. It should be drowned out by another voice in your head, the one shouting, "Whoopee! This is FUN!"

Chapter 1

Planning, Prepping, and Packing

• • • • •

When it comes to autism, spontaneity can feel like a big, fat "Don't." The days of last-minute decisions and let's-jump-in-the-car outings come to an end because predictability and routine play such a big role in equilibrium for a child on the spectrum. Planning and preparation are important, but you don't need to be handcuffed to your day-to-day life. Fun is often about pushing the envelope, doing new things, and moving outside the usual—and autism gives you a unique opportunity to do just that.

In order to get there, you need to do two things:

1. Identify the critical aspects of your usual routine that can (or must) be incorporated into any day.

2. Be prepared with tools to smooth over trouble spots.

You want to step outside of the ordinary. You know that you'll need to adjust when situations require it. But if you maintain some routines, it will help to create a feeling of stability. It requires some extra effort. Incorporating home-based routines when you are on the go can be a challenge. But the good news is that it becomes part of what bonds your family together, and it actually helps everyone feel grounded.

Routines that Matter

When you are deciding which of your routines are most important to maintain, you'll find that many of them involve meals. Food routines can be the most powerful and tenacious for kids with autism, and keeping your child's digestion and blood sugar consistent are foundational to a happy mood and fun day.

When you're on the go, try to keep food and mealtimes as close to your usual routine as possible. As tempting as it might be to hit a drive-through instead of packing a sandwich, don't sabotage your plans for the day with fried-food letdown and digestive distress if that is the result. Keep in mind that you are creating future expectations every time you undertake an outing. If you had a Happy Meal the last time you took a road trip, you might find you get flak if you don't do it the next time. So create routines you can live with from the start. Pack a sandwich or whatever works for your children and use purchased food as treats.

When it comes to style, small tricks can mean big points. If your child always eats his chocolate pudding with a certain spoon, toss that spoon in the bag. This you already know. But keep in mind too that more complicated routines (around washing hands or particular entertainment) can also be approximated. Since eating in a car seat while flying down a freeway is probably not your norm, resolve to take a fifteen-minute break and stop the car. Use a picnic table; take a bathroom break. The consistency points that you score will go toward keeping your child centered and happy for the more challenging aspects of the day.

Katherine, the mom of a six-year-old with autism, Aaron, and a typical eight-year-old, tells me, "I look at it as though Aaron has a certain set amount of tolerance to use for the whole day. We call them 'Aaron Minutes.' When the Aaron Minutes are gone, there is nothing to do but go home, because he is all used up and nothing will work out well. So we try to use Aaron Minutes where it counts. Even though it might be easier to stop at a sandwich shop for lunch, I pack homemade sandwiches on our favorite bread instead. That way we get to spend Aaron Minutes on our trip, not on convincing him to eat a Kaiser roll or whatever the sandwich shop might do differently."

Look at all of your routines with an eye toward portability. Andrea, the mom of a four-year-old, shared this experience: "We had resigned ourselves to the idea that Jason had to have the television on in order to eat. But it really tied our hands when we were out of the house. Either he wouldn't eat meals, or he would end the meals totally stressed out. Everyone was full of anxiety from getting through it. But one winter, we had a power outage at our house. We had to improvise. We used a battery-powered tape recorder with a *Blue's Clues* audiotape, and it worked fine. Then that tape recorder opened up a whole world of eating outside our own home!"

Don't be persuaded into cheeseburgers just because kids are begging. Mom and Dad know best. You don't have to explain that your child with autism has to have his plain turkey sandwich. Just tell all the kids that you've brought a picnic. It is just one of the ways you've planned a fun day.

You're So Preppy

Learning how to play the Preparation Game generally starts when you have a new baby. You learn to pack a diaper bag that can practically (or literally) give milk. You are ready for eruptions of body fluids in public, constant hunger, and a crazily shifting attention span. Grabbing the keys and dashing out the door becomes a laughable memory.

The difference between autism families and typical families is that the need to prepare like that doesn't fade so much as it evolves. Preparation may or may not continue to cover eruptions of body fluid, but it stays critical regardless. Just embrace it. Do you know the feeling that comes when you produce just the right distracter and ward off impending distress in a public place? It's a joyous reward. It can evoke a feeling of accomplishment like no other.

Before planning a trip large or small, know your little traveling companions. It is important to take everyone's needs into account. Think through your tools. Do you have a big bag that is comfortable to carry? If not, take the time to shop for one that you really like. It is an investment worth making. Look into bags with a cross-body messenger-style strap or backpack straps. They'll leave your hands free for kid wrangling.

In addition to your always-with-you bag, pack other bags that have different and specific purposes. For example, if you are going to the beach, pack clean, dry clothes in a separate bag from the one you'll be taking to the sand. You may decide to leave it in your car and change at the end of the day. When you know you will be picnicking, keep the eating tools and clean-up supplies in a bag that's separate from the food so it can be left behind in the car when the mealtime is over.

Keep a large cooler or thermal bag in the car stocked with cold drinks, snacks, and frozen ice packs (those ice packs can double for first aid if anyone falls down). Then bring a second, lunch-sized thermal bag and draw what you need from the big cooler for short forays.

Freeze a couple of water bottles (be sure to leave them partially open in the freezer and leave space in the container so the ice can expand), and freeze some foil juice bags too. You can use these instead of single-use ice packs in your cooler. They can do double duty as cool treats throughout the day. If your child eats yogurt, you can purchase freezable yogurt tubes, which also serve well in this capacity.

Pack a bag that always stays in your car. Stock it with a complete change of clothes, an extra pair of shoes, a few empty plastic grocery bags, some packaged, nonperishable snacks, sealed bottled water, undergarments or diapers, a packet of wet wipes, and any other necessities particular to your household. If you can actually spend one night away from home based on that bag, you've hit the nail on the head. That means you will have backup in any situation, and in any weather. Just don't forget to replenish what you borrow from that bag!

Develop a couple of different "Don't Forget" checklists and keep them on your computer. When you are planning a weekend away, a day trip, an overnight at Grandma's, or a week's vacation in a camper, you can pull up the right list and print it. Be sure to make changes to the lists as you find things that are needed or as your family's needs change.

Scouting Locations

When you have identified a destination, advance scouting can help make any trip go more smoothly. Start with the Internet. Confirm important information on public websites, such as the price of entry (and do they accept credit cards?), parking details, availability of restrooms, hours of operation, etc. Don't be shy about picking up the phone and asking to speak with someone about your family's needs. Most destination spots are eager to accommodate visitors with disabilities, but they don't always know what information to publish on a website. If you need to know something, ask. If you have an accommodation to request that would make a difference in your day, ask. The worst they can do is say no!

Following is a standard list of questions to ask when you speak with a representative from a destination spot. It can be your jumping off place each time you need to make this kind of call, and you can modify it over time as you discover the accommodations that are most helpful to you.

- Are there bathrooms near the entrance? Do I need to wait in line to pay for admission before being permitted to use a bathroom?

- Does your facility have family bathrooms? If not, ask if they'll understand if you need to bring your son into the ladies' room. Sometimes they can accommodate families with an older boy by making an employee bathroom available or by stationing someone by the door to help give you privacy.

- Am I allowed to bring my own food past the admission point? You may need to explain that your child has special dietary needs if they say no. The need to maintain dietary consistency due to an autism spectrum disorder *does* count as a special diet!

- Do you offer a discount for customers with a disability?

- Is it okay to bring in my own stroller?

- Do you offer special needs passes?

- Can I purchase tickets in advance to avoid waiting in line?

Many places will confide that they offer special needs passes or other planned accommodations but they don't like to put these on their websites because then "too many people would ask." Always ask at amusement parks, museums, aquariums, and other major tourism destinations whether they have such accommodations. Special needs passes can help you avoid long lines, loud antechambers, or restrictive rules that would inhibit your ability to have a relaxing day. A handicapped discount may reduce the price, but a special needs pass can provide accommodations to make a public attraction less difficult. It's best to ask by phone in advance so you don't need to make pronouncements or argue details while your children are standing next to you. Be sure to find out what kind of documentation or information they require to be permitted a pass. Some places will tell you that the only thing needed is a parent request; other places want a doctor's letter or some other form of verification.

But many parents feel guilty asking for a special needs pass and worry that they are being judged because their child with autism or Asperger's doesn't "look handicapped." Don't anticipate other peoples' prejudices, or worse, act on what you think people might say or think. There are plenty of difficulties and downsides involved with raising a child who has an autism spectrum disorder. If there is a convenience available that will help your family, don't avoid it or feel burdened by guilt about using it. Make your family's day the best it can be!

Parking

Although the requirements differ from state to state, usually families who have a child with a developmental disability are entitled to a blue handicapped placard through the Department of Motor Vehicles (DMV). Access to those reserved parking spots will help you traverse crowded parking lots safely and efficiently, especially when you have multiple children in tow. Contact your local DMV or use their website to check procedures and requirements.

If you live in a state that permits a blue placard for children with developmental disabilities, generally a doctor must sign the form. Be advised that some pediatricians may be reluctant to sign the form. Sometimes they do not understand the difficulties and dangers faced by parents when a child with behavioral problems is forced to walk long distances in crowded areas. If you run into that kind of resistance with your child's doctor, explain why it is necessary to help you manage safely, especially if you have other children you must protect at the same time. An alternative is to ask your child's psychologist to sign the form, as they are often far more in touch with the realities of autism.

Sometimes having access to a blue parking spot can make the difference between being able to go on an outing or staying home. If you believe it can help your family, take the time to go through the process. You won't be sorry.

When you have a blue parking placard from the Department of Motor Vehicles, it usually comes with a document to be kept in the glove compartment. Make a photocopy of that document and keep it in your wallet. It may prove useful when requesting special needs passes or discounts for customers with disabilities.

Getting Psyched

How does your child handle new situations? It's something critical to consider when planning outings big or small. Getting ready for any adventure requires emotional preparation along with the logistical preparation. You and your child need to "get psyched."

Will your child feel better if you explain your destination in advance and talk about details, or will that kind of discussion cause anticipatory stress or allow too much time for your child to build anxiety? Some kids handle situations better when the day unfolds without a big buildup. Other kids need to see what is coming in order to feel calm. You'll need to explore your child's best style and create readiness routines accordingly. If advance discussion is helpful, follow through devotedly.

But you should also be open to experimenting. From time to time, challenge what you think works best, because circumstances can change. Abby said, "We were using a visual schedule with icons that our home program agency suggested. It was helpful. But as my son got older, he started saying 'No' every time we put something new on there. At first we would change our plans, but then we discovered that if we just went without announcing it first, he was fine! So we did side-by-side tests, a few weekends in a row. First we announced our destination in advance and used the visual schedule, then we tried just heading out with a simple 'Time to go!' There was no denying that Jeff was much happier when he discovered our destination on arrival. We realized that telling him in advance was causing him to worry about things and form all kinds of fears. So we faded out the practice of using a schedule over the weekends, even though it still seemed to help at school."

Here are some other tools that you can think about for your "Getting Psyched" routine:

1. Plan ahead with a monthly calendar. Using a traditional wall calendar to mark an approaching event can be a nice way to build anticipation and share information. You can experiment with how far in advance to start.

Use it to start discussing the big-picture information and reassure about any nerve-inducing questions.

Karla says, "I made a calendar with Santino that we kept in the kitchen. When we unfolded the page to December, you could see the trip to see Grandma in red letters on the twenty-first. Together we added a sticker of an airplane, and I showed him pictures of the last time we went. Every night before bed we put a slash mark in the day that was over. Each time we did, he asked me about Grandma's house. Finally the day before the trip, we packed a bag of airplane toys and slashed out the last day. That whole morning went so much better than it had the previous year because it wasn't a surprise for him."

2. *Use an interactive schedule.* An interactive schedule is one that requires a child to do something as each item is completed. Sometimes it means placing an icon in an "All Done" pouch, or crossing out the item with a marker. It doesn't have to be fancy. If you already use a visual schedule at school or home that includes icons and a wallboard, of course you can expand it for family adventures as well. But if a daily schedule is not part of your routine, a simple, handwritten version can come in handy when something unusual is planned. Try different styles to discover what works, but start by keeping it simple. If it seems helpful, you can expand with pictures

plus words (or just pictures), icons or magnetic pieces, or the computer.

Althea, whose son is six, uses a spiral-bound notebook and two Sharpies. She makes big, open check boxes next to each item so her son can cross off things in a different color before moving on. She says, "It was really helpful when we started using the checklist schedule for outings. We talk through the schedule before we leave the house, and he tells me what he thinks are the best and worst parts of the day. I break things down as far as I can, because putting a big 'X' in the box when something is done is his favorite part. And afterwards, we use the checklist to talk over the day and remember what we did."

Other calendar styles to try:

- Portable version of a home icon board (where each item is removed from the list and placed in an "All Done" pouch as it is completed)

- To-do list application on an iPhone, iPad, or other portable device

- Picture board (great for a prereader)

- A notebook or three-ring binder that can be carried from place to place

Having a schedule can help your child see what is coming next, how long he has to wait for most-preferred activities, and gauge the length of a day. It is also a way to add anticipation to the end of less-desirable aspects like a long car ride. Siblings can help too—make them part of the schedule effort. You may find that they also like knowing what is coming next.

If you expand your schedule style, think about whether you'll be able to maintain it. You don't want to develop a system that is so elaborate that you can't or won't want to sustain it.

Stay flexible. Remember that there will be times when you need to add or remove things from your schedule without warning. You may forget to allow for a bathroom break but nature calls. Or perhaps there isn't time to stop at the grocery store on the way home after all. Be sure to leave room between line listings, have a way to shuffle and add, and think ahead about how you will remove items when you must. If those kinds of changes "on the fly" cause stress for your child, it can help to have a plan for how you'll handle it. You can try building choice into the schedule from the outset ("We will either go to the store OR go straight home") or try operating during those times without the schedule. Remember that its purpose is to relieve stress, not cause it.

3. *Tell Social Stories.* Social Stories are a visual way to share information about an upcoming situation or event. They can give your child advance information about what's coming in an accessible and pleasurable format, like a storybook. Your stories can give descriptions of what to expect as well as information on appropriate behavior when you arrive at your destination. They can be used to deliver complicated information and even instructions in a fun way.

Sherry uses Social Stories with her son all the time. "The first time I tried it was before a dentist visit for a checkup; I found a good Social Story online that walked us through entering the waiting room and giving our name, seeing the dentist, and getting a toothbrush at the end. Because it used my son's name and was about us, it seemed to help more than a character book about visiting the dentist had in the past. So we started using them often, both because they were helpful and because I didn't want Matthew to tense up whenever I pulled one out, like if I only used them for dentist visits and other big deals. I am not much of an artist, but I have drawn a couple of pictures freehand. I usually use Google Images! I put one image and one sentence per page, and we read it over a few times before we set out."

You can find a nice overview of Social Stories and also some tools for creating them at www.thegraycenter. org/social-stories/what-are-social-stories.

4. *Work through a reading list.* Take a trip to your local library or bookstore to get psyched for an outing or adventure. If your child does not do well with advance buildup, you don't need to call out the reason for the books you've chosen. But books are a great opener to introduce ideas and demonstrate what to expect. When characters are involved, it can create a sense of familiarity and comfort. There are books out there that prepare kids for events as routine as a visit to the dentist or as exotic as trips to the ocean. And don't restrict yourself to the kids' section. You can also look for grown-up books and magazines that have full-color photographs and practical information about your destination. If you are going rock climbing, for example, check out a copy of *Climbing Magazine.* Also consider buying some magazines that can be used for cutting out photographs. Then you and your child can get out scissors and make a collage of photographs as a fun way to prepare.

5. *Keep a journal.* Help your child cope with a new activity and process it afterwards by using photographs and captions to describe the events. You can use a cell phone,

a digital camera, or even a Polaroid camera to take snapshots throughout the day as events unfold. Later your photos can be assembled into a journal about the day. Your photo journal can be in mind as you proceed through the day and will become a terrific tool for sharing pleasure after the trip. As you build up history from previous outings, older photos can be used to gear up for a new trip that might have similar aspects.

6. *Communicate calm.* Getting psyched and being prepared comes with one last responsibility, and that is to communicate calm. It is important that your child learns to trust not only your words but also your actions. Spectrum kids pick up a tremendous amount of information from the environment, but they may not be able to talk about what they've observed. So if you are running around the house, loading up backpacks, making phone calls, and packing the car, your child will pick up that "something" is happening. It's okay to let your kids see that anticipatory excitement, but try to keep stress and jitters out of your tone. Anticipation is great—apprehension is another matter.

Knowing what will or won't work for your family is an important part of planning. There may be events or outings that just don't work. The idea is: Don't do those. There are going to be times when it is best for your family to split up and head for two different places, if something is important to one person that absolutely fails another. Bill, a father of three with one child on the spectrum, says, "My wife and I have learned that sometimes the kindest thing is to have two separate plans. My wife really doesn't like huge crowds, and my son Jack is with her on that. So if my daughters and I want to go to some event where we know there will be crowds, noise, a lot of walking, it is an easy decision. We split into two camps. I love those kinds of festival environments, so I take the girls. Susie and Jack go for a hike. Everyone is happy!"

Remember also that not everything has to be therapeutic. There is a pervasive tone surrounding autism that helping your child involves constant attention to learning and generalizing. But no one can or should live under constant obligation all of the time. Living is learning. You don't have to "teach" your child to absorb hated environments as some sort of exercise in desensitization. Most days will hold plenty of opportunities for coping practice without pushing it in. Try to take off your Parent-as-Therapist hat during family time. Everyone needs a break from that persona, including you. Perhaps especially you. Sometimes the path to fun is the path of least resistance. Choose what works, discard what doesn't. It is a simple formula but one that many parents forget to embrace with the weight of so many obligations sitting on their shoulders.

Chapter 2

Finding Your Way with Friends

· · · · · ·

After an autism diagnosis, there are adjustments to make in almost every aspect of a family's life. Many parents describe a feeling of "BA" and "AA" (Before Autism and After Autism) in their lives, with a bright line dividing the two. Relationships with family and with friends are especially touched by an autism diagnosis.

Most relationships will have to go through an adjustment period to adapt to the new information. Within families, everyone adjusts with differing degrees of success. Elders may never truly understand, and they may make remarks or hold ideas that really miss the mark. In those cases, it is the rest of the family that will have to do the bulk of the adapting.

Friendships are a different story. Each one comes with a different history, different kinds of attachments, and perhaps most importantly, different levels of willingness to adapt. Because people are usually not as committed to friendships as they are to family, if something isn't working or someone simply cannot understand autism, that friendship may slide away, never to be resurrected. That realization and process of adjustment can be terribly painful.

The first couple of years following a diagnosis are critical in reforming friendships or relinquishing relationships that don't work. At the same time, families living with autism should be forming new friendships with other families whose lives are affected. Those friendships are a great source of support.

One is Silver and the Other Gold

Even though it may sometimes feel like a lot of effort with dubious payoffs in the early days, try to keep old friends even as you make new friends. More experienced parents will remember that in the early days after a diagnosis, it is challenging to relate to people who don't understand what has happened to your life. Even more upsetting is watching friends juggle typical children and minor problems while complaining all the way.

But in time, those friendships and the typical children who are part of your family's extended circle will play an important role. And your child can play an important role in their lives too. Enduring through difficult times for future gain may seem like the last thing you want to do, but remind yourself that there will be a future filled with fun like playdates, birthday parties, and amusement park visits if the difficulties can be overcome. A peer buddy may become as important to your child as a good laugh with an old friend will be for you.

Dani tells this story: "One of my best friends wanted to be supportive when Eli was diagnosed, but she was saying all the wrong stuff. I felt like I needed her friendship, and I wanted her to listen, but she kept saying that she thought my son was fine and that it would all just blow over. I had to keep convincing her that my son really did have autism. Those conversations were the worst thing imaginable. But I stuck with it. I came to realize that she was going through a kind of denial that I couldn't allow myself to have. So we were out of synch. Eventually as Eli got older and she saw his difficulties more directly, I could talk about stuff like the kind of therapy we were doing. Our friendship survived. And it was worth it. Her kids are a source of support for my son at school and when we go places together her oldest boy looks out for Eli, which is huge."

If hanging on to a friendship is becoming painful, take a break. Even good friends (or perhaps especially good friends) can sustain some distance without creating a permanent rupture.

Take the Journey with Friends

Most families discover fairly early on that connecting with others who have children with autism can be a tremendous source of support. Through the autism community, you can do more than develop friendships—you can learn how to operate within the local support system and how to find better service providers. The Internet has been a huge help in connecting people with similar concerns. Take advantage of it. Start or join a Yahoo Group, and try Google Groups too. You'll find autism and Asperger's groups listed in the directory. Start at the top of the directory (http://groups.yahoo.com) and perform a search on your child's diagnosis plus your town or geographic area. You are very likely to come back with a ready-made collection of parents who have children on the spectrum. Other search terms to try are special needs, ASD, or specific terms related to the therapeutic approach you prefer (like RDI, biomedical, Floortime, or ABA). There are often national and local group options. As interesting as conversations may be at a national level, be sure to get connected locally. That will give you a chance to learn more about the kinds of activities happening near home and help you meet people who can identify with your day-to-day issues.

For example in my local parent group this week, I learned about a local movie theater running "Sensory Friendly Films," inviting families with special needs kids to come to particular matinees where the house lights will be kept on and the rules about audience noise relaxed. Several people made referrals to help a mom who was looking for a new speech therapist, and another person posted a notice about a new summer camp for kids with autism. Not bad!

You can participate in many more activities if you are operating with a group of families rather than as a single family. For example, if you visit a local skating rink during normal hours, you need to worry about the noise level, the music that might be playing, the hockey-skating boys slamming around on the ice, and a huge list of other fears that may or may not be realized. But if you approach the rink saying you represent a group of special needs parents and want to throw a skating party for special needs kids, you can ask about an advantageous rate for the group, arrange the environment to be more welcoming, and bring lots of families together for a good time. You go from being a parent who has an afternoon to kill to being a community organizer. Both roles have their place in your life, but if you can reach out to do some party planning and bring in a circle of friends, you are doing more than creating a fun day for your child. You are creating a fun day for lots of kids, a support network for their parents, and a feeling of community that is a balm for everyone's toughened skin.

Many businesses are receptive to hearing from special needs groups and willing to step forward with special events. But someone needs to be the catalyst. As long as each family pitches in the cost of admission, it is usually not hard to recoup costs, and if there is a surplus, it can be used to fund future parties or extras.

Here are some ideas for group events:

Gymnasiums

Local gymnasiums are wonderful spaces for special needs kids. The equipment offers variety and can be accessed by a wide range of ages and abilities. And they have experienced staff on the payroll. Developing a relationship with a gymnastics teacher might also lead to a regular weekly class or time slot for families if there is enough interest on both sides. Expect to spend around $300 to set aside time for a private party for your parent group. Usually a private party is between ninety minutes and two hours, but plans differ depending on the gym.

Bowling Alleys

Bowling alleys are by nature a location that might need some modification and public tolerance to work for kids with autism or other special needs. At first bowling alleys are loud, confusing places. But when kids have a chance to absorb and regulate, they'll hopefully see the fun. All this is best done among a group of like-minded parents and not under the glare of public eyes. Expect to pay around $400 for private time in a bowling alley. The availability and length of time differs between bowling alleys, so call yours for more information.

Ice Skating Rinks

Ice skating is a unique sport and some kids with autism have a remarkable affinity for it. But it does take practice and sensory adjustment. The air temperature is cold, the ice is cold, the movements are different. The echo can be loud. Like the bowling alley, a skating event without crowds of strangers and noise but full of friends and familiar faces is a great day. If you are holding a private party, often the management will allow lightweight chairs on the rink that kids can push for stability (and sit on when they get tired). Expect to pay around $700 for an indoor rink, perhaps less for outdoors. Contact your local skating rink to find out if they have plans or are willing to work with you.

Swimming Pools

The ideal swim environment for our kids tends to be an indoor, warm-water therapeutic swimming pool. These pools provide an amazing sensory experience and are fabulous for muscle development. With a staff of trained lifeguards, this would be the perfect place for a family event.

Inflatable Rentals and Party Destinations

Lately a crop of facilities have sprung up that offer a party spot filled with inflatable bouncers and slides. These are great for kids' birthday parties and are set up to work for kids of many ages and in groups. Since kids on the spectrum tend to adore these physical and sensory smorgasbords, some are even offering weekly or monthly parties for kids with special needs. If your local Bounce House is not already offering that kind of special needs family time, try approaching them about having a party where everyone kicks in to make the total payment. If things go well, they may want to expand to do a monthly event for families at less busy times.

If there is no inflatable party place near where you live, consider renting an outdoor bounce house or inflatable slide with a group of families just for fun. These tend to be reasonably priced and so even just a handful of friends can pick one out and use it for an afternoon. It needn't be a birthday party; it can just be a fun thing to do. Different bounce houses and slides have different pricing, but expect to pay around $100 for a bounce house for an afternoon.

Keep your eyes out for other local venues that would be fun for a group party. Look in local free newspapers or magazines targeted at parents, which tend to display lots of birthday party ideas and other kid-friendly attractions. Birthday party venues and corporate staff getaways tend to be great settings for group functions because they already have the staffing and ideas arranged. But don't be intimidated if a venue that looks interesting doesn't seem obviously set up for a group. Pick up the phone and call the manager. The worst they can do is say no. And as the old saying goes, nothing ventured, nothing gained.

One parent visiting a location with a child who has unique needs is a single customer. You'll find that if you fit into the way that particular place does business, you'll have a successful customer relationship. But a group of families together looking for recreation for their families is a more powerful entity. Together you are a group that businesses want to attract. If you approach as a collective and ask about things like group rates, special times for visits, or accommodations that would help create a great visit, they'll be more interested in working with you. So build your friendship network knowing that not only will you be arranging emotional sustenance, but you'll be positioned for real-world rewards as well.

Chapter 3

The Happy House

· · · · ·

The most important environment for your child is the one you create at home. It is the place where you have the most control over how it works and how it looks, so your challenge is to design spaces to meet everyone's needs. Don't fall into the trap of thinking that your place is too small to be fun or that all rooms must be used for the purpose intended by the builder. Small is workable, and your home's architect probably knew nothing about raising a family coping with autism.

Remember too that "all fun, all the time" would be like living in a theme park. Your home needs to offer not only excitement but also respite and calm. You'll want an arrangement that allows your home to be an exciting place when that's needed, but also a soothing retreat when the world's slings and arrows send you or your child running for cover.

Your first responsibility is to forget about *HGTV* and *Better Homes and Gardens*. If those kinds of images come into your head when you think of a terrific home, you're designing for another family (one that eats neatly at mealtimes only and tiptoes around on white carpets.) Is that your family? Is that any real family? You want to be able to use your home and enjoy it every day, not admire its beauty from afar.

You're Getting Very Sleepy...

Your child's room needs to be quiet, calm, and serene. It is not unusual for kids with autism to experience sleep difficulty at some time or another. Getting past that may be as simple as putting a consistent bedtime routine in place or as complicated as dietary changes or medical intervention. But the physical state of a child's room is also very important. It's easy to forget that our mood is affected by our environment.

Be careful about laying a child down at night in the same room that he played in boisterously (or had intervention therapy in) during the day. Those associations will remain even when the lights go out. Instead do what you can to set the room apart as an island of tranquility.

If your child shares a room with a sibling, the same concepts apply. A calm and distraction-free room would help anyone sleep better. But if it is possible for your child with autism to have his own room, it will be easier for you to tailor the environment to his needs.

Keeping the room restful and calm does mean banishing terribly exciting toys. If it flashes, beeps, talks, or races around a track, it should live somewhere else in your house. You can still use bedroom storage space wisely. Look around the house for toys, games, or items that your child tends to ignore. If you want to use storage space in your child's room for toys, these less-preferred items are the ones that should be put there.

Lori says, "My son has no interest in stuffed animals. But my daughter Kylie has a whole zoo of stuffed bears, tigers, bunnies, every animal you can think of. During the day she plays with them all the time. But at night we toss them in a huge basket in Jake's room. Jake's trains get put away in Kylie's room. It sounds backwards, but it works. During the day they visit each other's rooms to find their favorite stuff and sometimes they play with each other. At night the toys aren't temptations for either of them."

Try to avoid using your child's room as a therapy setting during the day. Even though your child's therapy may be fun some or all of the time, sometimes it is also exciting and sometimes it is hard work. Regardless of the day's choices, it is almost always going to be stimulating in some way. The atmosphere you want for therapy is one that promotes engagement and awareness. But that's the opposite of what you are going for when it comes to designing a sleeping place.

Look around your child's room with a critical eye. The bed may have the blankets or body-sized pillows that work best. But are the pictures on the walls tranquil? Or did you choose them for their fun and appeal? If you've hung images or characters on the walls that excite your child, think it over. Thomas the Tank Engine or Lightning McQueen may be cheerful and enticing in the daytime and may express your child's personality among friends. But at night they may be acting as a window into a world that doesn't promote sleep. Consider calming images instead, such as beach photographs or framed maps.

Take a last look around. Sleep is critical for your entire family, so do what you must to create the right sleep atmosphere in your child's room. Does he turn on the lights and stay up until all hours? You may need to unscrew the light bulb. Does he get into the closet and make a mess of your off-season clothing and storage items? Perhaps you need to put a lock on that closet. Once the room's purpose is clearly felt and sleep patterns are regular, you'll feel more interested in enjoying the rest of the house and expressing a sense of fun there.

A Balancing Act

Now that you've created a calm and soothing environment for sleep, it's time to look around the rest of the house for fun. As you walk through your rooms, don't worry so much about what the house seems to call for. You don't need to arrange or choose furniture and accessories because the space seems to require it. It is more important to choose items because they work for your life.

Luckily most modern families have already discarded outdated ideas about furniture arrangement. We've stopped maintaining pristine living rooms for guests to use but where kids are not allowed to play. And you can keep going. If you've got a room set aside for entertaining visitors, think about returning it to usable space for your family, at least until your kids are older. You may have to rethink the way you accommodate guests, but the benefits could outweigh the downsides.

Tracy says, "When Mark was a baby, I loved having a guest bedroom so my mom could visit on the spur of the moment. I decorated it to be welcoming and restful for her. But we really needed the space! So I got rid of the spare bed, which took up most of the room, and we used it as a play/therapy room. It had a big impact on our family room! Now that the kids had that room to themselves, I felt more able to reduce the clutter where we watched TV, and it felt much more peaceful there. We have a spare bed in the garage that my husband can drag in when Mom comes to visit, and overall it was worth the trade."

One of the biggest challenges you may face is creating spaces that are attractive for everyone—adults as well as a child seeking sensory input. You can create rooms that include sensory exploration but are not so radically adapted that you feel as though you are relaxing with family in an occupational clinic.

"Our family room has couches and a TV like you'd expect. But we keep at least one sensory item for Adam in the room too. When he loses interest, we rotate. His favorite is the air mattress. Sometimes we inflate it tight, sometimes mushy. Adam loves to lie on it and squish around. But when he loses interest, we put it away and bring out a weighted blanket, or the vibrating massage chair pad, or the faux fur rug. We've found that if the room stays interesting for him, it translates into more family time."

On the other hand, some parents become so devoted to adaptation that their own needs are subordinated. Even though you are striving for fun and may be willing to allow the unconventional, it's important to set boundaries and maintain spaces that look and feel like grown-ups can relax there. Bill says, "We have two rooms in our house where no toys are allowed. One is Mom and Dad's bedroom, and the other is the family room where our main television sits. The kids can bring their things in and play there, but they take them out again when they are done. There are some drawers and closed cabinets where toys can be kept out of sight. And in the evenings, when the kids are in bed, my wife and I sit and read, talk, or pay bills. Having the boundaries has had a good impact on our kids too. They've learned that different rules apply in different places. My wife and I like to feel like actual grown-ups after a day of office work and child wrangling."

It Don't Mean a Thing If You Ain't Got a Swing!

You probably already know about the sensory benefits of swinging. It can be calm and soothing or exciting and alerting. Many kids with autism are happiest in motion, so a swing is one of the best gifts you can give. And if you are under the impression that swings only make sense outdoors, think again! Swings can be terrific indoors, if they are used for gentle, rhythmic swinging, as opposed to the all-out boisterous swinging, which is best kept outdoors.

Just don't make the mistake of putting an indoor swing in a room that is largely used as a sensory room or gym. It can be tempting—after you visit an occupational therapy clinic where they have a variety of swings, gym mats, and tons of equipment, it is easy to come home thinking, "We could have that at home!" Some parents do go ahead and re-create those settings, turning a garage, basement, or spare room into a gym. That has its benefits, but it can also lead to a division in family time. Often the result is that the room where your child is most comfortable is not the same place that your family wants to congregate.

Instead try hanging the swing where your family likes to be. If you tend to relax in the family room, hang the swing there. Your child may not be interested in the same television programs that others want to watch, but he'll be sure to stick around for the swing. That leads to the couch, and together it all translates into more time together as a family and more opportunities for hugs and squeezes. If your child is off seeking sensation and input in a separate room, opportunities are lost. Having a swing in the family room doesn't have to conflict with the idea of having a room that feels grown-up at the end of the day. If the swing has been hung with a carabiner, it's easy to take down. Or a discreet hook on the wall will allow you to pull the swing off to one side when it isn't in use.

Hanging an Indoor Swing

Hardware stores carry weight-bearing eye screws that cost less than five dollars. While you are there, you'll need a stud sensor to help you locate an overhead support beam. If you are fortunate enough to have exposed beams (or partially exposed beams) in your ceiling, you'll know right where to start.

Attach an O-ring with a screw closure to the eye hook. Keep in mind that every piece you use to hang a swing must be rated to hold sufficient weight. The entire apparatus is only as safe as the weakest piece. Once you have the ceiling hook ready, you can begin collecting an assortment of swings to switch frequently. Climbing carabiners are a big help. If one begins losing its zing, you can unclip it, put it away, and try a different one. You can fill in holes with wood putty and paint over them when it comes time to move.

Recommended Indoor Swings

- *Hammock chairs.* These provide maximum support so a child can completely relax while in motion. They are a great way to neutralize challenges and promote calm. Our current favorite hammock chair came from Hammocks.com, but there are great deals to be found all over the Internet.

- *Flat-bottomed swing.* IKEA makes a terrific and inexpensive model with a smooth wood plank bottom. It requires more participation from its passenger than the hammock to balance and hold on to the side ropes. It takes further organization to propel the swing into motion. A terrific challenge.

- *Soft-bottomed swing.* Like the flat-bottomed, this one requires a lot of participation from the passenger. Instead of a hard, flat seat, there is a wide, soft strap of rubber. It requires a slightly different set of movements and balance, so putting it into rotation adds fun and novelty. Toy stores often carry these for under $30.

- *Lycra "hug" swing.* This one is easy to make and positively indispensable. Purchase 3 yards of Lycra at a fabric store. Pick one with a fairly tight weave and less elasticity than your average bathing suit (so your child won't drop to the floor when he climbs in). If you can find velvetized Lycra, it is less stretchy and nicely opaque. Tie a knot in each end of the length of fabric. Put a carabiner clip (not a fashion accessory, but one designed to bear sufficient weight) under each knot and then use a third carabiner to join the first two together. Hang the swing from the ceiling by that third carabiner. Once your child learns to crawl in, he will be hooked. It's like a cocoon in there, delivering pressure on all sides. When you add motion to the feeling of total enclosure, it creates a complete sensory escape from the world. When your child is inside, you can spin it to create additional tightness, and then release for a dizzying ride.

Carabiner clips can be found in sporting goods stores (those that sell climbing equipment) and many hardware stores. If you find them at a bargain price, buy a handful. They'll come in handy with many of your swings. Always check the packaging to be sure it is a weight-bearing model, since some carabiner clips are ornamental. Carabiners have become fashionable as everything from key chains to jewelry. If the package is silent about the weight it can bear, keep looking. That means it is not designed to bear any!

Keep the Principle of the Swing in mind as you place the other play equipment around your house. Does it remove your child from where everyone will want to sit and relax? Look for a spot that won't lead your child into finding the best sensory stuff away from the family.

Small Bounce

Since they are designed for adult exercise, mini trampolines are entirely able to handle a child's weight. They provide a great outlet for kids to release some big energy indoors, and they can be dragged outside when the weather is nice. Put the trampoline where you work or where your child's siblings are most likely to play. The mini-tramp is plenty of fun right out of the box. But for a change, throw a soft, rubber-backed bathmat on top to deliver a different sensation to the bottoms of the feet.

You don't need to spend hundreds of dollars at a therapy supply house for a mini-trampoline. You can find them for around $30 at a sporting goods store. It's not a good item to pick up used, because the general lifespan is only eighteen to twenty-four months, and you don't want someone else's wear-and-tear to jeopardize your child's safety.

Always keep an eye on safety. If an indoor trampoline gets a lot of use, it will show signs of wear. Watch for fraying or peeling in the fabric that covers the springs, wobbling feet, or exhausted springs. If parts start to go bad, replace the whole tramp with a new one. A hand-me-down in good condition is worth a try if you want to decide whether a trampoline is right for your child. But don't push the envelope with one that looks shot.

The Best Nest

Have you looked behind your couch lately? Go ahead. It might need a quick pass with the vacuum if you haven't been back there in a while. Move the couch away from the wall. If you can put a three-foot galley back there, you've created a refuge. It is naturally nearly enclosed, small, and safe. With a soft rug or fuzzy, rubber-backed bathroom mats and some favorite toys, you've got the perfect retreat for a child under ten with autism.

One mom reports, "Kevin loves the area behind our couch, we call it his 'apartment.' He listens to music and reads books back there. We've hung some fabric on the wall and put a bunch of pillows back there. It's like his own little nest."

Indulging Interests at Home

Professionals don't always agree on the best way to handle intense interests. Some recommend limiting or denying access to a fascination, but others will tell parents to allow the pursuit at home, hoping to provide enough satisfaction so that the child can leave it behind when it is time to go out. Each family has to decide how much (or if) they will allow intensely preferred activities.

One family I know came to the conclusion early on that in their son Dylan's case, fighting his strong pulls would turn their family time into a battleground. Given the strength of his attraction to certain activities, simply transferring his interest to something else seemed like the only available victory. But as Stephanie, his mom, explained to me, "Then 'something else' would need to be put away too."

They decided to accommodate his interests at home but set boundaries. Dylan loves television. Not only does he want to watch, he wants to touch the screen and control the channels too. Before long, getting through even one program as a family was a struggle. Stephanie was constantly calling out, "NO TOUCHING!" Dylan would step back, but after a few minutes he'd come forward and repeat the cycle.

They tried an out-of-reach method, putting the TV on top of a tall wardrobe. It seemed to work for a time. But soon Dylan adjusted his efforts. Stephanie began finding chairs and stepstools piled in front of the wardrobe. She had to rethink the problem because she was worried he would get hurt climbing toward his goal. And when Dylan learned to use the remote control, new issues came to the fore.

So Stephanie purchased an old television set at a thrift shop for $20 and added a VCR for $7. She set up a closed-loop system to give Dylan access to his own collection of videotapes (but no access to cable or an antenna). She reports that it worked beautifully. It satisfied his desire to push the buttons and control the screen. She brought the family television back to eye level and enforced a rule that no one was allowed to touch it. When temptation strikes, she can redirect Dylan to his own "entertainment center."

Finding harmony is a challenge, without question. And it almost always involves compromise. But denying an intense interest can usher in a series of conflicts between you and your child and also between your family and your child. Remember to keep peace in your thinking. In the long run, if you put therapeutic principles over family harmony, the result may be siblings who feel resentful, contentious family time, and more misery than necessary. Accommodate, examine, and improvise. Think through your child's goal. In Stephanie's situation, her son didn't want to disrupt the family. He wanted to stop and start the images on the screen; the television was an irresistibly tempting machine. She found a way to give him his desire without sacrificing everyone's pleasure. Sometimes you have to create redundant systems or dedicate space and time to an interest that only one person has. But you can accommodate obsessions in livable ways. Make sure everyone feels reasonably satisfied with the solution. If one member of the family is harboring frustration, it will very likely burst forth eventually, or worse, become long-term anger.

The Hot Seat

Massage chairs can be very expensive, into the thousands of dollars. But don't let that discourage you. If you think a massage chair would be a good idea if only you could afford it, check out a massage chair pad for a fraction of the cost. You can find these at an electronics store or on Amazon by searching for "cushion" under Health & Personal Care › Health Care › Massage & Relaxation.

Massage chair pads can be placed on top of any chair or couch, and they can lay on the floor too. In addition to different vibration settings, some get warm to boot.

Inflated Expectations

You may already have an air mattress in a closet, but if you don't, they are easily available and fairly inexpensive at big-box stores like Target and Walmart. They are terrific sensory play tools at home and can be changed simply by varying the amount of air you pump in. In addition to rolling around on it, when it contains less air you can squeeze it into small spaces or up against walls for fun, and kids will enjoy it alone or with a parent. Try adding a blanket or sleeping bag for more sensory play.

Be sure to get a small electric pump along with a twin-size air mattress. You'll be able to fill the mattress in a jiffy. You can move it into different rooms for a change of perspective, make it "tight," or release air to make it squishy. And when the kids start taking it for granted or stepping over it without interest, put it away! Next time you take it out, it will be fun all over again.

Expanding the Boundaries of Bath Time

If your child loves the bath, you are not alone. Many kids on the spectrum love water. The bath is a huge opportunity for fun, especially when kids are small. I'm sure you have already explored water toys and bathtime books, bubble wands, and crayons or paint made from soap. If not, check out the child/baby section of a toy store, and prepare for some big fun!

But don't be bound by what is packaged and suggested for the bath. Opportunities for fun in the tub are everywhere. In addition to the bath-toy aisle, you can find waterproof toys all over the toy store. Unscented shaving cream, water balloons, squeaky toys, and car wash sponges are all fun in the bath.

Bath time is not only a cleaning imperative. A bath or shower can be a rainy-day activity or a good way to reset the mood after a tantrum or disappointment. Somehow everything feels better after a bath. If your child is recovering from a negative experience, use the tub to smooth the rough edges. And if your child is restless during a day spent at home, start that tub running.

Hot and cold water play is great sensory exploration. You may already have seen your child changing the water temperature from hot to cold and back again in the tub. That's an opening for you. It means changes in temperature are welcome and pleasurable, and that can be fun. Be sure to check your home's water heater for an adjustable temperature gauge. You should turn it down so that hot is never, ever scalding.

Try filling a regular spray bottle with cool tap water. While your child is lying in a warm bath, spray a light mist of water into the air overhead, and let it settle on bare skin. Wow! If he likes the feeling of the water in the bottle when it comes from the tap, try putting the spray bottle in the refrigerator so the contrast is even more dramatic.

Ice cubes are another great bath toy. Bring in a bowl and let your child play. Touch, taste, and temperature are all heightened by the contrast between the warm water in the tub and the frozen ice. Use baby-safe soap and don't worry if a little gets swallowed. That's just part of the experience.

Does your child like a soft, fluffy towel and a rubdown after a bath? Try heating his towel in the clothes dryer and putting it in an insulated bag or cooler. It will stay warm until he's ready to get out and be enveloped. Sensory heaven.

Playdate Activities at Home

Having another child over or encouraging play between siblings builds social skills and connectedness. We know that. But expecting kids to play together spontaneously is not always realistic. Play equipment and toys help, so the swing, trampoline, and other favorite toys in the house are good tools. But a great way to see these playdates take off is by leading the kids into a structured activity that includes everyone.

Here are some playdate ideas that can be used among your own kids too—not just when someone "special" comes over!

Talent Show

A video camera is a terrific tool. The kids can have a talent show, read poems, recite the alphabet, or act out roles complete with costumes—whatever is within their reach. Even if you just record some general activity and play it back, it will attract everyone. The finished product will be fun for your child's friends to take home and show their families.

Photography is another great way to capture fun. You can set up sequences and photograph each step, then challenge the kids to arrange the photos in the right order. Or set up a craft project like making picture frames out of Popsicle sticks, which will lead to a take-home treat for friends.

Treasure Hunts

Make index cards with pictures or word clues for locations around the house, such as the couch, the bed, and the bathtub. The kids will have to go to the pictured places to find the next clue. The last clue can be the kitchen table where a treat awaits as the prize!

For kids who can read or spell, describe each location with a series of clues ("The place where we get the mail"). For variety, put pieces of paper with letters (or Scrabble game tiles) in some locations. The kids will have to decode the letters to spell the next location. Icons, line drawings, or photographs can be substituted for kids who are not yet reading.

Old Faithful

Did you know that if you drop a Mentos candy into a full 2-liter bottle of Diet Coke, it will create a geyser that shoots 2–3 feet in the air? Now you do! Take this one outside. It will be a sticky mess, but it will be fun! Don't forget the countdown to heighten anticipation.

Pin Jockeys

Make your own bowling set by saving empty water bottles and having the kids fill them with tap water. Use food coloring to perk up the water. Try different balls until you find the right one. Since the bottles are full, you'll need something with a little weight. A big rubber playground ball (the kind used to play four square) should work well.

Making Food

Cooking is always great fun, and it uses a variety of technical and interactive skills (assembling ingredients, measuring, stirring). Best of all, it ends in a delicacy. Try these Colorful Cakes.

Colorful Cakes

1 box white cake mix and required additional ingredients as described on back of the box

1 box food coloring

Cupcake baking pan

Paper liners for cupcake baking pan

1 can white frosting

Various cupcake toppings (some suggestions include sprinkles, M&M's, raisins)

Kids take turns adding ingredients and stirring the batter. Pour the plain mix into individual bowls and let each child choose colors for their cakes. Colors can be mixed too. When the batter is done, pour into a cupcake pan lined with cupcake liners.

While the cupcakes are baking, enjoy a different activity, preferably an active one. Try sending the kids outside for an obstacle course or a relay race. (Relay races are terrific because they involve a cooperative effort as well as a competitive one. Make sure to celebrate that everyone participated as much as, or more than, who won.) If you are needed outside to supervise these activities, make sure you remember the stove is on! Bring a portable timer with you that will make a big noise when the cupcake cooking time is up.

When the cupcakes are finished and have cooled a bit, round up the kids again. Give each child a small bowl of white frosting. Choose colors again and stir in. Ice the colored cupcakes with the different colored icing, then decorate with toppings. You can let the kids create unique designs or suggest ideas such as faces, numbers, self-portraits, or characters.

A simpler, healthier alternative to cupcakes is smoothies. Cutting up the fruit, the noise of the blender, and the yummy reward are all good experiences the kids can have together.

Right In Your Own Backyard

Backyards are a huge opportunity for fun, no matter the size or the climate. But they also come with challenges as your child gets older. There are a wide variety of plastic toys for climbing, sliding, and bathing when kids are toddlers. But when a child outgrows those, what comes next? If you believe the advice of mommy magazines, you'll be spending big money on swing sets and redwood climbing structures. These are both terrifically expensive and require a lot of space. And who knows if your child will get long-term enjoyment out of them? It's a risk. You may be better off leaving structural pieces to public parks and school playgrounds. Think instead about what isn't available nearby.

If you have room in your yard for a full-size trampoline, give it some consideration. Your family or friends may gasp at the idea, but that usually means they don't have a child on the spectrum and don't understand what it's like to live a life of all-out sensory adventure. Full-size trampolines are major fun. If you've only ever tried a mini-tramp, you may have a mistaken idea about the big brother. Mini-tramps are firm and strung tightly for indoor safety and adult weight expectations. An outdoor trampoline is a completely different beast. It is much spongier, more elastic, and thrillingly reboundable. It is an intense full-body experience.

When you consider that absolutely every child you know will be eager to jump on it too, you'll have a kid-magnet with huge sensory benefits right in your own backyard. One mom, Carolyn, reports that she saw tremendous gains in her son's attention and regulation when they started jumping every day. "Those gains were actually side benefits to the great times we have singing, counting, jumping, and being incredibly silly up there," she said.

If you are considering a trampoline, always factor in the cost of the safety sides. These are nylon nets that surround the trampoline on poles that stand about five feet high and affix to the base. These sides prevent bouncers from encountering the springs with their feet as well as falling off the trampoline over the side. They may be presented as "optional" by stores and websites, but they are definitely not optional. Not only do they increase the safety of the trampoline by a huge factor, they also increase everyone's feelings of comfort. The same is true for a padded cover for the springs. Keep an eye on Craigslist, local want ads, and Freecycle, because trampolines are like pool tables: hotly desired when the space is available, but difficult to unload when their time has passed. Inspect a used trampoline carefully, and don't take any chances on questionable equipment. Make sure no one has been bouncing on the trampoline with shoes on by inspecting the surface for holes or tears.

Games are great on the tramp, but remember to leave all props on the ground. No musical instruments, flags, or any other accoutrements belong up there. Everyone's pockets should be empty too. The risk of mishap is too great, and the fun is plentiful without those things.

Steer kids away from competitive games on the trampoline ("I can jump higher than you can!"). You don't want anyone pushing the envelope up there. Cooperative games are safer and will help you keep things under control as the spotter. They'll also keep the playing field more level for various abilities. Have kids move around the trampoline in the same direction. Don't be afraid to call for a time-out if someone is getting too rowdy on the tramp. Whether it is your own child or a neighborhood pal, it is your job to keep the play under control. Enact house rules that no one is allowed on the tramp without permission, and there must be an adult watching. You may discover that older kids from the neighborhood want to negotiate exceptions to your rules. You might be tempted, but be smart and stand firm.

Here are some great games to try on the trampoline with kids:

- *Ring Around the Rosy.* Simple, classic, and always a winner. Try the second verse: "Cows are in the meadow, eating buttercups. Thunder, lightning, we all stand UP!" Lather, rinse, and repeat.

- *Countdown to blast off.* Jump to the numbers beginning at 10 or 20. Try a sit bounce or a loud cheer when you come to the end.

- *Jump rope rhymes.* These are terrific, rhythmic, and perfect for jumping along. All kids like alphabet rhymes, but if you've got a hyperlexic child, he'll be hooked. (Hyperlexia is a fascination with numbers or letters that sometimes comes with autism.) "A my name is Annie and my husband's name is Albert. We come from Alabama and we sell Apples. B my name is…" You'll find websites with great possibilities if you Google the term "bus songs."

- *Rolling.* Lie down on top of your child and roll together across the trampoline surface. The softness and give of the canvas makes this game much more fun on the tramp than on grass. Pressure, closeness, and motion, what could be better?

- *Categories.* Pick a category that interests your child (cars, foods, animals). Each person names an item in that category that starts with the last letter of the previous entry. (Mom goes first and the category is Animals. She starts with "Elephant!" Johnny's turn is next. Because elephant ends in "t," he says: "Tiger!" Then Jane says "Rabbit." Then back to Mom ["Tarantula!"] jumping all the while.) The categories can get more specific and challenging. Incorporate everyone's interests.

Most importantly, get up there on the trampoline with your kids. You'll be surprised by how good it feels. Standing on the sidelines cannot take the place of the connection that happens when you are both flying in the air together, holding hands.

The Outdoor Swing

Having a swing in your house doesn't mean you are done hanging swings. The inside swing serves a different purpose from the outdoor version. Gentle, rhythmic swinging in the house is soothing, but outdoor swings provoke much more excitement, speed, and challenge. Walk around and look up. Are there any places where you can throw a rope over a strong branch? Always use a weight-bearing rope that you buy new.

Put a carabiner clip or make a round loop at the end of your rope so you can change swings easily. All the swings in your indoor catalog will seem new hanging from a tree. Try them all even as you collect other, more active possibilities. Here are some to consider:

- *Disc swing.* A round plastic disc at the end of a rope is a new physical challenge. Getting on takes balance and upper body strength, and staying on requires trunk muscles. Standing on it is the next step for the more advanced or older child. These are around $25 at larger toy stores or online.

- *Elastic rope.* All your swings will feel like new if you use a piece of bungee rope in the hanging. Spring Swings makes a disc swing with a bouncy rope that turns back-and-forth into an up-and-down affair. It can be combined with other swings if your kids enjoy it.

- *Trapeze.* It uses a different set of muscles and is a ton of fun! Definitely not an indoor swing. Be sure to supervise with this and all your swings at all times.

- *Tire swing.* Great for social swinging and families with multiples. Don't try to use a real tire, which can be dangerous and incredibly dirty. Tire swings tend to be more expensive than the other choices, but they do offer a different perspective, especially if you have siblings or neighbors who will regularly want to share.

More Backyard Fun

If you still have room and trees to spare, try a zip line. This is an outdoor toy that stretches between two trees. It has a carrier that glides across the line. Zip lines are easier to install than they look. The wire wraps around the trunk of a tree at either end, so it is adjustable for both the size of the trunk and distance between the trees. Riding the zip line takes some practice and more strength than the swings. But the purpose is immediately visible and the payoff looks fun. Hopefully your child will be willing to put some energy into mastering it.

Another great piece of backyard equipment is a stationary bicycle. A stationary bike is an excellent tool for a child who has not yet mastered bike riding. It reduces the challenges to pedaling and holding on to the handlebars while sitting on the seat. There is no need to balance, steer, brake, or use judgment while in motion. The skills can be acquired in stages, and a sense of accomplishment comes much sooner.

Shop in second-hand sporting goods stores and thrift shops. The simpler the stationary bike, the better. You want to be comfortable leaving it outside. Try to avoid multiple buttons and electronic readouts—those are too distracting. Make sure that the seat and pedals can be adjusted for a small rider.

The next step would be a regular bike with training wheels. Bikes of any size can be outfitted with training wheels. From there you could take the training wheels off together or one at a time. But whether your child is new to biking or already riding, a stationary bike in your backyard offers safety, independence, and exercise.

When summer comes, sprinklers, Slip 'n Slides, and other water toys can't be beat. Get together with a few friends and each buy a different one. Then you can rotate the toys around so the variety stays high and the price stays low.

If you allow your kids to play with a hose, be sure to buy one safe for potable water. The water coming out of the usual style of green garden hose is absolutely not safe for consumption. And you can be pretty sure that on hot days, plenty of water will make it into the mouths of playing children. The potable water hoses are usually white and made from material that won't leach toxins or chemicals into the water.

Getting Stumped

The next time you drive by some guys on the side of the road with a power saw surrounded by pieces of a big tree, stop the car! Tree stumps are versatile and fun. Try to get several of similar (but not uniform) size.

Arrange the stumps in a circle and plant them firmly in the ground. Standing on top and hopping from one to the next is a fun balance challenge.

Duck, duck, goose is just right too. And how about a drum circle? Everyone can play an instrument or bang on a drum along with some music. The kids can use the stumps themselves as noisemakers or bring drums or other instruments outside. Make your own music or play along with a boom box.

Place a bucket in the middle of the circle and give everyone bean bags or small pebbles from the ground. See who can toss the most into the bucket. Was it too easy? Try a cup. You can change the receptacle and the tossing item to make the game new or more challenging. Was it too hard? Try a larger or shallower bucket.

There are plenty of fun activities for kids sitting in a circle, so encourage groups to gather. Listen to music, play guitar, toast marshmallows, pass a hot potato, read a book aloud and pass it every few paragraphs. Keep everyone in the loop while sitting on their own stump. That's what makes it fun.

Keeping Heart in Your Home

Whether you're hanging swings, collecting extra pillows for fort building, or pulling couches out from the wall, feel the home's balance. As tempting as it might be to tilt everything for your child on the spectrum, it wouldn't be best for him or the rest of your family. Siblings can join in the fun. Make sure that you maintain perspective at home and reflect all the people who live there. You have interests and ideas that include your spectrum child and some that do not. Accommodate where you can, examine the possibilities, and improvise solutions. Your goal is not only to help your child feel fulfilled and happy but also to help everyone at home feel that way together.

Chapter 4

Finding Community Fun

· · · · ·

In any community there are activities and locations designed for family entertainment. Every day, families make use of duck ponds, malls, ice rinks, swimming pools, and other spots. Most can work for a sensory-challenged child too, even if they need some modification to really succeed.

Thinking ahead and planning well are key factors in creating local fun. Especially when it comes to nearby and inexpensive attractions, an advance recon mission to scope out the location and find trouble spots will serve you well. Does the snack bar at the bowling alley only offer food that your child isn't allowed to eat because of a special diet? Does the skating rink play music that is way too loud?

Often parents have a short list of good things to do in their own neighborhoods. But it is all too easy to fall into a pattern of visiting the same resources again and again without realizing there are other fun experiences just waiting to be had. You don't need to endure the same old playground unless it happens to be exactly where you want to be. And even if it is, you can bring along one or two tools to boost the fun, like a water gun, a kite, or a wagon to ride in.

Kristen says, "We have a neighborhood playground where we go all the time. It works well because my son is used to it, and we could bug out quickly if things weren't going well. But last summer we made a date to meet a friend at a park near her house, and I was amazed watching my son have such a blast on the different equipment. That was when I realized that the rigid routine was mine, not Daniel's!"

A great first step is to simply make a project out of visiting all the different parks in your town (and neighboring towns). Usually they have different equipment and layouts. There is a huge benefit to discovering that your children enjoy a variety of different playgrounds instead of sticking to one or two in particular. There are playgrounds and public parks everywhere you go in the United States, so whether you are visiting Grandma and Grandpa two hours away or traveling for a vacation, you know you'll find a setting that works. If you start by getting to know a variety of playgrounds in your home area, you'll find that you can successfully visit new parks and playgrounds whenever you are somewhere new. And though parks have different features and equipment to explore, there is also a feeling of sameness that comes with them. You tend to see a central climbing structure with monkey bars, sometimes swings, all placed over ground cover like sand or a soft surface to prevent falling down injuries. That familiarity is comforting in a strange town. And for parents, it is great to know there is a location the family can visit that will feel somewhat familiar and be fun regardless of what other resources are available.

If you have an iPhone, there's a free app called "Parks." It identifies your location using GPS and then shows all the nearby playgrounds and public parks. It is a terrific tool if you are heading down the highway and find that everyone needs to get out and stretch. Or you can use your home computer to simply look for green areas on the map. And many towns list local parks and their general features on their website. You might compare notes with other families; find out which ones are their favorites and share yours. Heather said, "One summer we made it a project to visit a different park in the area every few days. Finn and I got to know them all, and it was a huge advantage for us ever after!"

Getting Ready

Before trying new activities, it is a great idea to show your kids a video of the activity in action. You can build interest and familiarity by watching other kids or favorite characters enjoy the setting. Getting a feel for an environment in two dimensions will help to smooth the experience for kids on the spectrum. If you visit a location for an advance reconnaissance mission, bring a video camera, flip video recorder, or even use your phone to take some photos so you can show your child what it is like. If you cannot film a location or activity, check YouTube; you may find that someone else has posted what you need.

Ice Skating

Sometimes ice skating is a surprise skill for kids with autism. Once they understand the adjustments it requires in balance and they get a taste of the feeling of speed, it becomes huge fun. Check local yellow pages for ice rinks in your area. If your community doesn't have any rinks nearby, skip ahead to the next activities in this chapter for plenty of other opportunities for fun around town.

If you or your child is worried about falling while ice-skating, check out a used sporting goods store for protective elbow and knee pads designed for hockey. You needn't get the full regalia, but covering trouble spots can increase everyone's feelings of confidence. Once your child learns that he won't get hurt and that falling is just part of skating, he'll begin to let go of the wall and try to glide.

Consider the hurdles you'll encounter on your way to the ice. Begin by knowing your child's shoe size with confidence. When you step up to rent skates, you'll need to tell the person behind the counter what size you need. Keep in mind that thick socks will add to a foot's bulk, so measure at home with the proper socks already on your child. The thick socks will help to keep feet warm and comfortable against what is probably a stiffer-feeling leather than what your child is accustomed to, so don't forget them. Bring an extra pair of socks in case the leather feels particularly uncomfortable or your child has a half-size foot (most rinks only carry whole-size skates).

There is a nice tutorial on measuring shoe size along with charts to translate inches into standard sizes at http://shoes. about.com/od/fitcomfort/ss/measurefeet.htm. You can do it at home with a piece of paper so there is no need to fuss with loud stores and cold metal foot-measuring devices that require a child to stand still and allow a stranger to fiddle with his legs and feet.

On your way to the rink (and this is true of the bowling alley too, which we will delve into soon), wear a style of shoe that is easy on and off. It will minimize your time and trouble in the changing area. Of course your child probably already wears easy on and off shoes to minimize trouble throughout life!

Bring a large tote bag with your supplies, snacks, and a bottle of water. Skating is a surprising amount of exercise, whether you are good at it or not. If possible, leave your valuables and wallet in the car so you can feel at peace leaving your bag in the changing room while you go on the ice. Some rinks have lockers but most tend to expect people to shove their bag under an open wooden bench.

If you'll be entering the rink from a very different outdoor climate (such as a warm summer day), be prepared with cold weather clothes to layer on once you are inside. Gloves are an absolute must. The first time your child reaches out to touch the ice, you want to be sure it is a novel and interesting sensory experience and not a burning or frightening feeling. He may insist on taking the gloves off and touching the ice directly, but he'll be ready for that if he starts with protected hands.

Unless your child has a serious aversion to wearing a hat, bring along one or two that you can put on. If a woolen cap is too close and feels too strange, even a baseball cap will help to keep the child warm and protected and is worth having. If you live in a climate where hat wearing is not necessary, you may have to compromise on the style or length of time he'll wear it, but give it your best shot.

Many skating rinks have a changing room that can be crowded or echoey. If you can minimize the time you spend in a difficult environment, you'll be best off. When you walk in, stake out an area where you can prepare to skate, and then go to it.

Many rinks have "Special Skaters" programs for kids with disabilities, so you might call to find out if there is such a program locally. If not, ask them about the best times for you to bring your child. They know their schedule and can tell you when it is least likely to be loud and boisterous. Weekend open skating hours tend to be packed with kids having a great time, and for a new or less-confident skater, the careening hockey players and whirling figure skating students can be scary. If you can go for the first time during a weekday morning, those times are generally designed to accommodate older adults and serious skaters practicing their moves. It will be quieter, and they may be willing to accommodate your requests for music—or no music—if one or the other would help your child. Once you have been a few times you'll be able to consider those weekend hours since the experience will be familiar.

To get ready for a trip to the skating rink with your child, try searching on YouTube, Amazon, and at your local library for videos and books. Introduce the idea of skating by starting with the aspect that you think will interest your child most. Will the feeling of moving fast and feeling the cold (in other words the sensory aspects) be the key factor? Or perhaps the science of ice rinks, how they work and are maintained, will be the most interesting way to start. Hockey and figure skaters make great visual examples, and a Social Story is easy to create.

Roller Skating

Roller rinks still exist in some towns, and they offer some advantages over the ice version. For one thing, they are not as cold! And you can practice skating in a driveway or park before entering a rink. If your child is used to wheels-on activities like biking or tricycle riding, the whole idea will be less of a radical change than strapping on blades. Depending on your child's age and size, you may be able to start with either inline or quadline skates. The elbow and knee pads will again come in handy here, and a helmet is not an unusual sight at a roller rink. A recon trip to size up the place and assess the challenge would be well worth the time if you can drop in while your child is at school. Again, you want to talk to the employees to find out the best times to find the rink less populated. A crowded roller rink can be very loud.

Bowling

Bowling alleys can be found in almost any town or nearby location, so bowling is also a nice activity to try. The noise level is the first thing to consider in these places, since it can be considerable. If you are concerned that the noise will be a problem for your child, you might go to the bowling alley a few times with no expectation of bowling. Often they have arcade-style machines with prize-dispensing capabilities, so going in, eating some french fries, watching the bowlers, getting a prize, and leaving is a very successful outing. And once you've tried that, you can advance to things like picking up the balls to see how they feel, watching the balls roll back to the starting point, and writing on the score-keeping machine. If the bowling alley also has a billiards area, consider putting some quarters in the pool table and letting your child push the balls into the pockets while he gets used to the environment. Keep expectations low on your first outing!

Most alleys have guards that will block off the gutters for young bowlers. These can really add to the sense of success. But you'll need to ask them to put them in place, a process that is manual or automatic depending on the lanes. Many bowling alleys can let you use a ball ramp as well, which lets the child simply push the ball, launching it down the ramp and into the alley with minimal effort. Since the ball is heavy, especially for a kid, you'll have to experiment to find the system that works best for your family.

At the bowling alley as well as other destinations, don't be shy about asking for accommodations that would help your child—especially if you have taken the trouble to make an advance visit to the venue, come during a low-traffic time, or do your part in making things go with a high probability of success. The staff will often cooperate; they generally want to help make things more fun for your family. So if there is grating music blaring in the background, go ahead and ask if they'll turn it off or down. If having the front door propped open means your child will be attracted to the exit, ask the manager on duty if you can close it. Usually the kinds of accommodations that help kids with autism haven't occurred to people who have no experience in that department. Changing them can be a simple matter. Speak up about what would make your family's adventure better.

Another way to improve an experience is to use off-season thinking. When the weather is cold out, everyone thinks about going ice skating. But ice skating is plenty of fun at an indoor rink in the summertime, and an even more powerful sensory experience to boot. Find out about off-season times for activities that interest you, and go when no one else is thinking of it. It may mean swimming when it is cold and skating when it is hot—but that is part of the adventure if that is what makes it work.

Massage Chairs

Have you ever noticed a line of massage chairs at your local mall or electronics store? Don't pass them by. See if your child would like to try one, either sitting on your lap or on his own. Need an outing to eat up some time on a rainy afternoon? Try making a visit to some coin-operated massage chairs; they often have these at the local mall.

Party Places

Around the country, more and more children's party places have sprung up. One of the most successful is the inflatable party place. These large, indoor spaces boast a variety of inflatable jumping structures, from the standard jump house to the wilder obstacle courses. Check the Appendix for a listing of some national party chains, but check your local listings as well, in case there are some owner-operated locations.

These places can be huge fun for kids with autism, sometimes just as they are, sometimes with some accommodation. Find out if they offer any "free play" time where anyone can come in and jump. If not, you may need to gather a group and set up a party to use the space. If a group splits the cost, it is not too expensive.

Sometimes these places are very loud, on account of the noise of the fans maintaining the structures as well as the elated children and loud music. If that is a problem for your child, ask them to turn off the music. Make sure your child is wearing comfortable socks, since no-shoes-but-socks-on is usually the rule.

Gymnastics Facilities

Some gyms have game courts for basketball, but the kind of gymnasium parents of kids with autism should look for is the kind that teaches tumbling to kids interested in cartwheels, back handsprings, and balance beams. These gyms often have experience teaching children with special needs, and their equipment is tremendous fun.

For example, at the Gold Star Gym in Mountain View, California, they have several trampolines, springboards, a foam pit, and acres of floor mats. They also have experience with young kids and kids with special needs. Since they offer birthday party packages, they are already equipped to hold private group events. Any interested group of families can get together and use the space to hold a party for kids, even if there isn't a particular birthday to celebrate. When everyone pitches in, the cost is reasonable, and a gym is a great place to play, especially during rainy months.

Visit the websites of gymnastic facilities in your area. Speak with the manager about the best way to bring kids with autism to the facility, whether it is with a group event, a class, or a free-play time.

Pooling Your Resources

Swimming is an incredible activity for all kids, but most of all for kids with autism. The benefits are so wide and far-reaching that many parents consider it an indispensable part of their interventions. But swimming is just as essential when you are looking for fun and adventure with your child.

Start by finding out about local facilities. Make it your business to know about all the pools in your area, the warmer the better. Indoor pools are important because they translate into consistent, year-round access. Outdoor pools are subject to the season, but they provide greater access and a much more social environment. Keep an eye on your local paper in April and May, or search its online archive if it has one. Papers often publish a list of local swimming locations at the beginning of summer, and you can clip and keep it for year-round information.

Swimming proficiency is excellent exercise, and in a young person's world that is often dominated by team sports, swimming offers an environment of individual achievement combined with social fun. If you can interest your child in swimming, it will pay off with its overall conditioning, sensory, and social benefits.

While it is best to start with individual lessons to help your child gain confidence and proficiency, transition to group lessons as soon as possible. If your child doesn't respond well to the instructional aspects but enjoys being in the pool, be willing to let the lessons go in favor of free swimming time. It is important to separate the joy of swimming from the potentially less fun aspect of taking lessons. If your child loves both the activity and the instruction, that is great. But if he loves the activity and dislikes the lessons, drop the lessons in order to preserve the fun. Most swimming pools and recreational facilities offer free swim times and allow patrons to swim even if they are not actively engaged in instruction or swimming on a team. The benefits of swimming will remain in place even if your child participates only for pleasure and not with structure.

Most importantly, put on a swimsuit and get in the pool with your child! Swimming together is a terrific activity. It is a game the whole family can play. Almost all children love swimming, so it is an activity your child will be able to share with siblings and friends. But the way to teach your child that swimming can involve social interaction is to be part of it yourself.

Foraging for Food

After an outing like ice skating or swimming, you are bound to have a pack of hungry children on your hands. The availability of gluten-free and casein-free food in markets is improving, but what about restaurants? Happily, GF and GF/CF options are also becoming more available on menus. Many families who try these special diets had all but given up on being able to eat out or grab a prepared meal quickly and easily. Being able to find readily available restaurant food is fabulous and helps to make everyone feel less deprived.

Here are some national chain restaurants that offer GF/CF menu options or GF options that can become CF with substitution or restriction. All chains ask that customers explicitly check with their local restaurant to verify the status of selections and to discover if any new items have become available.

- Boston Market

- Chevys

- Chilis

- Outback Steak House

- P. F. Chang's

- Subway

- TCBY

In addition to keeping a mental list of your usual errand places (places your child will tolerate or even enjoy that will kill some time on a slow afternoon), look around for stores that offer a unique outing in and of themselves. Is there a local music store with drums and instruments that you can try? How about a visit to a sporting goods store that has exercise machines on hand to try?

Angie says, "We have a huge furniture warehouse in our area that my son adores. The people who work there are really nice, so we browse on rainy days, trying out the couches and twirling on the office chairs. Brian and I can spend a couple of hours there and even grab some lunch in their cafeteria. It is a great rainy day activity."

And Marilyn discovered, "There is a Turkish rug merchant in my town who has a store that feels like Ali Baba's cave. Once I happened in there with my son and they could not have been more welcoming. Now every once in a while we go for a visit, and James climbs on luxuriant piles of silk rugs or lets me cover him with a rug for the pressure. Of course we never do any damage, but we don't buy anything either. Someday when I can afford it, I will take my business there because they have been so great to us!"

Some kids get a kick out of big hardware stores like The Home Depot, where they can explore different plastic pipe pieces or wander through aisles of plants and nursery trees. The bigger the shopping carts the better, because a child can sit inside the cart and enjoy the ride. Keep an open mind as you go about town and think about how to turn ordinary locations into fun ways to play.

Summertime

Summer can be a particularly long and challenging time for autism families. With school on hiatus or operating in reduced hours, time weighs heavy on our hands. Adding to the problem is the difficulty of finding a summer camp that will accept and work with your child's needs.

Summer programs tend to be minimally staffed, often with young people whose experience with kids is limited to these camps. Sometimes such programs are reluctant to accept kids with disabilities, or they may accept kids and then not know how to make it a successful experience for them.

Start planning for summer as early as you can. If you haven't found a local program that works for your child through your school or by talking to other parents, contact your local Department of Parks and Recreation to see what they offer. As a division of the local government, these programs are not permitted to discriminate on the basis of disability. That said, they may not be prepared to handle a child with special needs. Find out what their experience has been with other families and if they are openly willing to work with you. It may be as simple as making sure your child's group has an additional counselor at the ready to enhance the child-to-adult ratio, or they may be able to assign an aide to your child specifically. Sometimes the people who work during the school year as aides are eager to find summer work, and you can make that connection, leading to a familiar face for your child.

Look in particular for programs that have a central element that your child enjoys. If swimming is a year-round pleasure, a camp with a pool is the place to start. If Lego blocks are a big interest, there may be a camp that focuses on that activity.

Camps run by religious organizations or private companies have more flexibility when it comes to accepting or turning away campers. Ask among fellow parents if any in your town have a good reputation for being accommodating. Generally speaking, don't try to remake an uncooperative organization. If a camp is unwelcoming or has a poor track record in the special needs community, don't burn energy trying to change them. If they've made it clear that they don't want your child to attend, the likelihood of it becoming a fun program after you've insisted is low.

If you have been unsuccessful at finding a summer program for your child, you're not alone. It is a frustrating situation for many parents of children with autism. There just aren't nationally run programs for kids with autism such as are found in other special needs communities. You may need to draw on your parent network. Chances are good that if you can't find anything, there are other local families in the same boat. Perhaps two parents of children with similar profiles can pool their resources and hire a private aide who can attend camp with their two kids. Or perhaps you can gather a group and create a schedule among yourselves. Mornings at the park, afternoons at the public pool, rotating parent supervision. In the end, you may make a better summer program than anything the Department of Parks and Recs has to offer!

Visiting Your Hometown

Try to look at your own community as if you are a visitor. You may be surprised to find resources that you never knew existed. The Web offers rich veins of information, such as the website for your local Chamber of Commerce, so you can explore and discover new possibilities without leaving your home. The better you know your own town, the more fun you'll have there!

Chapter 5

Comfortable Clothing for a Fun Life

· · · · ·

Since sensory issues so often go with the autism spectrum, most parents learn early on that they need to give some extra care to choosing clothes for their kids. Removing tags and hunting for 100 percent cotton are just the start. There are a variety of challenges that require parent attention when it comes to choosing clothes for our kids. When you are using your free time to chase fun and adventure, you want to be dressed in the most effective and comfortable ways. And on top of that, clothing presents some important clues about the wearer to the world. Parents of kids with social challenges have to create a wardrobe that is first and foremost comfortable and workable, but which also helps their children seek out fun and friendship.

Creating Your Shoe Menu

Shoes can be both the trickiest and most important item to figure out for a child with autism. You need to consider whether your child can tie his own shoes, whether his feet are wide or narrow (or neither), and whether shoes can contribute to a reduction in toe walking or ameliorate any gait challenges.

Since tying shoes is a fine-motor challenge for any kid, shoes with Velcro closures are a godsend. They are a great way to promote independence and sidestep (so to speak) a potential problem. Velcro shoe straps are increasingly popular and easily found when children are young, but as kids get older, availability diminishes. Some styles are still around, but the array of choices is reduced.

The popular online shoe store Zappos.com offers an amazing selection of shoes plus free shipping on both deliveries and returns. They take a lot of the pain out of shoe shopping for parents whose kids don't like stores and may resist trying on multiple pairs of shoes in one session. You can order a few options or a couple of different sizes and try them on at home when it is convenient, over a few days. Then you can return any that don't work out. The return process is painless and you can print postage-paid address labels from the Zappos.com website. They also have the benefit of a well-designed search engine, so you can narrow the field based on various (and sometimes unusual) criteria. If you are looking for Velcro closures on Zappos or any other site, the key term is "hook and loop." Try searching on that with your child's shoe size to get the most matches possible.

One brand that is terrific for kids who need easy on and off shoes is Vans (www.Vans.com). In addition to having great skater-boy (or skater-girl) vibes, they make styles with Velcro closures in all sizes. They also have a classic slip-on sneaker in a variety of edgy designs, from flames to skull and crossbones. Vans have a tendency to run wide, so if you are experimenting with orthotics or other shoe inserts to address toe walking, these are a good choice. Scott Yamakoshi of Kidsteps Pediatric Therapy says, "I also suggest Vans for my kids who wear leg supports because they have that extra room."

Many children on the spectrum walk on their toes and for different reasons. It may take some investigation and several tries to find shoes that help, if any will. If your child is seeking sensation for the bottom of his feet, orthotics or shoe inserts can assist. You can buy different types of inserts at the drugstore and cut them down to size before investing in something custom made. Try gel inserts for extra squishiness. If craving input is not the reason for the toe walking, then shoe inserts (and custom orthotics) probably won't lead to change. But since they are inexpensive, why not start there and see if they help?

It may be that a child who toe-walks needs extra support in his ankles. Ariana says, "We tried everything to get our son Johnny to walk on his feet, with no success. Then he added a funny ankle bend to his walk, so we looked for high-top shoes to counteract the ankle dip. Wow! Not only did the ankle dip stop, he came down off his toes for about 75 percent of the day. It was a huge difference and we were really happy. The only problem was that then I had to keep finding high-top sneakers with Velcro closures!"

Ariana passed along that her greatest success was discovering wrestling sneakers at sporting goods stores. They come in big-kid sizes, are terrifically lightweight, and are designed to provide good traction. And best of all, they come in styles with Velcro closures that look very cool. Google search for "wrestling shoes kids" to see what they look like and compare prices.

During winter months, it becomes easier to find boot styles with Velcro closures that provide lots of ankle support. Lightweight hiking sneakers are a particularly good option. But as weather gets warmer, it can be tricky to find shoes that give ankle support, aren't too hot, and look reasonably cool.

Some kids find that regular sneakers feel too heavy, causing them to drag their feet, remove their shoes, or otherwise modify their gaits. If finding super-lightweight shoes is your challenge, check out styles called "water shoes" that are designed for beach and underwater wear. These tend to be extremely lightweight as well as having easy-on styles and closures. If you find them at a discount store like Walmart or anywhere else at a reduced price, pick up an extra pair to keep in your car. Water shoes make great "just in case" shoes since they tend to be super-stretchy and are puddle-proof. They won't be outgrown as quickly as other styles, so keeping them in your car (or at school) will take you further.

Shoe fashions will always come and go, and in recent years there have been two particular crazes which stand out: the Ugg style of sheepskin-lined boots and the Crocs fad of plastic, colorful clogs. Following fashion is a low priority for families who prioritize fun and extreme usability, but both of these fashions have some possible benefits. And as other companies jump on the bandwagon, they create low-cost alternatives and parents can win out.

Sheepskin-lined boots are a nice alternative for a second (or third) pair of shoes, especially if your child enjoys variety. Some kids tire of wearing the same pair of shoes each day and try to create their own variations by changing their gaits. To avoid that kind of "fun," keep more than one pair of shoes on hand and offer your child a choice in the morning. Allowing him to choose may also give you guidance on future purchases. Boots with a soft lining don't make a good everyday pair (because they lack arch support), but they feel extraordinary as adults have discovered too.

Soft, enveloping, and warm, they are a sensory treat that you can offer without a lot of hassle. Easy to pull on and off, not necessarily requiring socks, and rugged for a kid who is active, these boots are a nice addition to a shoe menu.

Even though Crocs are very popular and offer lightweight and easy-on advantages, they tend to fit too loosely for most children. Some kids won't keep them on or will find them too distracting. In the last year or so Crocs have come out with styles that incorporate better support than the original clog, so you can look for those in addition to the more recognizable style. If you find that your child likes plastic shoes and can wear them successfully, Crocs (or Croc knocks, look-alike shoes by other manufacturers) are another great spare shoe choice as well.

How Many Feet You Meet

A last note about choosing footwear for your child: Look for socks that have contrasting color patches on the heels and toes. Manufacturers use these markings to emphasize the wonderful reinforcement built into their socks. But for children who are putting on their own socks and shoes, those socks with contrasting heels and colored stitching provide important visual clues to the correct orientation. It represents a small choice to make at the store, but it can have a big impact on independence.

One Leg at a Time

If finding the right pants for your child has become a head-ache, head to the Land's End website (www.landsend.com). They have great elastic-waist cargo styles to choose from for both boys and girls, and they offer sizing for slim, husky, and regular kids. If you have a long, lean, little guy, this is the place to find cargo pants that reach the ground and not just his ankles. It is also a great place to find soft jersey pants with a cute flair for girls. And if you are trying to avoid the look of "plumber's pants," fit is the key. Keep an eye on their "Overstocks" tab because they do start discounting when limited sizes of an item are in stock, and some great deals show up. Finally, if you order something from Land's End that isn't as expected or what you hoped, you can avoid return shipping charges by taking it back to a local Sears. They accept returns on purchases made online right in the store.

Regardless of where a child is when it comes to the potty-training ladder, pants that require fine-motor manipulation can present a challenge. Whether a kid is fully trained, schedule trained, or still working toward a bathroom goal, elastic pants add ease not only for the child but also for caregivers who may be helping. Fortunately these styles are as popular with typical kids as they are with the parents of kids with autism, so your child is likely to fit right in.

Sweatpants and track suits are a staple in a great many wardrobes too, but for a sensory-aware child, take the extra step of looking for styles that 1) have an elastic band instead of a drawstring on the waist, since tying a drawstring is difficult and it can be uncomfortable, and 2) have open hems on the bottom. Many sweatpants embrace a style that includes elastic ankles, and this is a place on the body where elastic is not your friend. The cuffs tend to ride up and grab the calf, causing discomfort and sometimes irritation. If you have trouble finding soft, unstructured pants that don't include ankle grabbers, look in the night-wear department. Solid-colored fleece pajama bottoms can double as track pants, especially for weekends or time around the house. Pajama bottoms in solid colors also wash easily and have a roomy fit, so keeping them your spare "car" pair of pants works well.

Rochelle shared, "I was having a really hard time finding plain old sweatpants that didn't grab at the ankle because Billy hates those. I finally just bought a pair that had elastic, but in one size up. I cut off the bottoms when I got home, and they were perfect."

Scissors can be a good friend when it comes to maintaining a comfortable year-round wardrobe. Since most parents are buying several pairs of pants during the school year (to keep at home, to keep in the car, to keep at school) there is no need to buy as many pairs of shorts when the season changes as well. When spring comes around, take out the stack of pants that still fit in the waist. Set aside a pair or two for cooler weather and nights, or any that look as though they might make it through another year. Then take scissors to the rest!

When you cut off pants into shorts, be sure to leave them an inch or two longer than you intend as your final result. You can buy a product called Stitch Witchery in any sewing or variety store; it is an iron-on, no-sew tape. You can even order a roll online at Amazon.com. Just place a length of tape under the turned hem of your cut-off pants, cover with a damp towel, and iron. Your child will then have a large collection of new shorts that are nevertheless comfortable and familiar. And you can wait until autumn to start the whole cycle over again! This no-sew hem job works on virtually all pants, including track pants and sweatpants. You don't have to be Martha Stewart to do it, either. Less than an hour with an iron and you are done.

Getting Shirty

How cheeky you want to be on your kid's T-shirts is a decision best made by considering individual factors such as how well your child understands the slogans on display, how well he can handle the kinds of reactions those slogans might provoke, and the tolerance in your community. But generally speaking, staying away from the controversial is a good policy.

But T-shirts that correspond with your child's interests can help him connect with others. So keep your eyes open during the course of daily life for shirts that display a logo for where you swim, a great local museum, your favorite pizza place, or a revered superhero. Teachers, peers, and other people in the community can use these tidbits of information to form a connection or start a conversation.

Some sources for kids' T-shirts:

- Disney—www.disneystore.com

- Shirt Crazy Kids—www.kidsonlyworld.com

- Shirts4Squirts—www.shirts4squirts.com

- Zazzle.com—www.zazzle.com/kids#kids

If identification is an issue for you, consider adding name tags to your child's shirts. These are inexpensive and easy to apply (get out your iron again). You can buy iron-in nametags easily and inexpensively at www.irononcamplabels.com. Or you can use a permanent and nonwashable Sharpie marker.

Carefully consider the information you want to provide on your child's clothing. Using a cell phone number can be a great way to go because it can outlast family moves and transcend vacations. Providing too much information can present a hazard if your child is likely to trust strangers easily. Always mark your coats and outerwear at least, as those items cost more and are easily misplaced. And if you are planning a more ambitious adventure and want to be sure your child has identification, look into temporary tattoos. If your child has a food allergy or medical condition, you already know that medical ID is a must and you can get a medical tattoo that reflects the problem as well. But even for a child who is at risk for getting separated from parents, a temporary tattoo can provide peace of mind. They make custom versions that can be designed with both safety and fun in mind. Put one on all your kids so no one is "singled out." Stray Tats creates custom tattoos in smaller quantities that might be fun for your whole family (http://straytats.com). For extra security, apply it near the left wrist. That's where medical personnel reach first to take a patient's pulse.

Have you noticed the hoodie craze in recent years? For parents of kids with autism, hoodies are even more than a fashion statement. That hood that seems to hang uselessly down the back of the garment is the perfect "handle" when you are out in public with a child. Especially as boys get older, they may not want to hold a parent's hand in public places. Certainly their typical peers reject "the hand" after about age six or seven. You can allow your child that same freedom even as you acknowledge the possibility of poor impulse control. Use the hoodie! You can gently hold on without him even knowing, certainly without the rest of the world paying attention. It gives you an added measure of security in crowded or potentially hazardous areas. And the great part is that all his peers are wearing hoodies too, so they are available in fabrics that range from lightweight shirts to sweatshirts and sherpa-lined sweatshirts. So be sure your child has at least one in his wardrobe that is the right weight for the season.

And for pullover-style hooded sweatshirts, a quick cut with a pair of scissors at the neckline down the front can really increase the comfort. Look for sweatshirts that have no elastic or relaxed elastic around the waist and cuffs as well, since those can be points of discomfort.

Water World

Swimming and water-related adventures require some extra thought when it comes to wearables. Each year you need to assess your child's water wear and make sure you are prepared. Between growth and the punishment that swimsuits take, buying them fresh every year is usually required.

A racing-style bathing suit is a good item to own, even if your child prefers to wear shorts in the pool, as most boys do. The racing suit makes a great underlayer if you are not 100 percent confident of potty issues, especially in a strange pool. They are essentially invisible and comfortable and easy to manage in a changing room. Swimoutlet.com has a great selection of kids' swimwear, and you can keep an eye on their T-shirt section for fun swim-related shirts as well.

Many stores now carry rash guards, which are shirts designed to be worn both in and out of the water along with swimsuits. They protect against sunburn and bugs, and they are a must-have for any child spending time outdoors, at a pool, the beach, or a waterpark. It is far more comfortable and usable than continually refreshing sunblock, and the protection from burn is much more effective. It is also far easier to cover up and forget the issue than it is to chase a child into shady areas or slather with lotion after each and every swim. They come in both long-sleeved and short-sleeved versions. When you are shopping for a rash guard, it can be a good idea to select a bright or somewhat unusual color. That will make it easier to spot and track your child at public pools or beaches.

If you pursue water activities that warrant a serious look at a wetsuit, like surfing, kayaking, off-season trips to the beach, or jet-skiing, shop around for the best price. Having a westuit can open up even more terrific water time in spring, autumn, and even winter months when everyone else is confined to land! The racing suit that you use as insurance under swim trunks is also the perfect undergarment for a neoprene wetsuit.

Getting It Right

The most important thing to do when choosing clothing for a child who may not express opinions of his own is to look around. What are the other kids his age wearing?

When kids are very young, large chain stores (like Gap or Old Navy) tend to present clothing that appeals to parent and grandparents. After all, that's who is buying the clothes. Kids are just along for the ride, and mostly they'll cooperate with what is made available.

But as they get older, many kids start expressing their own ideas and interests through their clothing. If your child is not interested in choosing his own outfits (at the store, at home, or both), pay attention to what other kids are choosing for themselves. Do the other boys at school choose a brightly striped polo shirt on a regular Monday?

Save fashion-forward, sweet, or adorable looks for family events and holiday celebrations. Allow everyday wear to reflect the fun, silliness, and childishness of being a kid. Let the kinds of interests that are representative of your child's age group take center stage, along with comfort and wearability. It is tempting to reach for the same kind of striped or sweet gear that appealed to you in the past. It is still available in larger sizes, because grandparents are still looking. But don't let those mall-ready looks dominate your child's overall wardrobe, even if some pieces are sprinkled in. A Spiderman T-shirt may not be to your taste, but it will speak to the other seven-year-olds in your child's life much more than anything with a polo pony on it. That kind of connection is much more important and more fun for your child than following fashion. Do something important for your child: Take wardrobe cues from peers.

Chapter 6

Grandparents, Extended Family, and Special Friends

. . . . .

Even if a child's grandparents are not part of his life, there are other adults who need to learn how to create a relationship with your child. It may be an aunt or family member who is willing to trade kids with you at times but needs help connecting, or a neighbor or friend who wants to get to know your child but doesn't know how. Sometimes family and friends have had no experience at all with autism and are afraid to invite your child over without you, fearing they won't know what to do. Try to take a lead role in helping them bridge the gap. And when all else fails, mark this page prominently and "forget" this book at your friend or relative's house.

When grandparents live nearby, activities and fun times may not differ much from what parents would plan. Local grandparents need to choose activities and outings that are within their physical ability, which may limit the options somewhat, but when they are a frequent presence in their grandchildren's lives, that familiarity provides a big edge.

It is a different story for out-of-towners. Visiting family can have difficulty forming a connection with a child who responds differently than they expect. It may be challenging for them to find fun ways to spend time with a child who has specific or unusual needs. The success or failure of time spent together depends heavily on their willingness to reach out, and their ability to keep reaching out even if they don't get the response they are accustomed to expecting. It is important for parents to give extended family and friends encouragement and appreciation when they are trying, whether they seem to be finding success or not.

To Grandparents, Aunts, Uncles, and Friends

Don't expect the child's parents to do all the work of connecting you with this child. A relationship cannot be formed for you prior to your arrival and transitioned over when you visit. It is up to you to discover ways to interact with the child and to ask questions that will help facilitate a relationship. Assume that everyone wants to help you form a bond, but they cannot do it for you. Your time, interest, and effort are the key tools that the situation requires.

Ask Questions

Before an out-of-town visit happens, ask about the child's overriding interests of the moment. Don't wait until you arrive to find out that he loves trains, the Teletubbies, or swimming, or that he has been horseback riding every single week since you last came to visit. If you have that information before you arrive, you can be prepared to use it to form a connection. Don't assume that your grand-child can interact with you on a general level until you find specific mutual interests. When a child has autism, inter-acting is one of the hardest things for him to do. But if you are familiar with his interests before you visit, you can visit his world successfully.

If, for example, you learn that the child you are visiting loves the Teletubbies, you needn't be discouraged if you don't know what the Teletubbies are. Your first stop should be to your local bookstore. A clerk can show you picture books associated with the interest. It doesn't matter if the interest is a category, a character, or an activity. There are few fascinations that a child can have that will not be represented at a book-store. Whether you want to buy a book associated with that interest as a gift to break the ice, or you just want to browse to get yourself up to speed, you will come away with a better understanding of the preoccupation.

Don't settle for the answer if you're told that this child "isn't interested in anything." It is possible that his parents have become so accustomed to watching his pursuits day in and day out that it has stopped seeming worth mentioning. But indeed, watching television is an interest. So is pulling leaves off trees, jumping up and down on a trampoline, or flipping a rubber toy in the air. It's what you *do* with the knowledge that makes the difference. Probe gently if information doesn't come easily. What does your grandchild like to do when he first comes home from school every day? What is his favorite thing about weekends? What will he do if you give him an hour of free time? Listen carefully to the answers. No activity or interest is too small. Everything he loves to do has the potential to be an opening for a loving connection.

So Now What Do I Do?

Once you know what your grandchild is most interested in, you need to find a way to use the interest as a jumping-off place. Your grandchild may not have the language skills to talk to you about his interest, but if you approach him with a basic understanding, it will help you bond.

Bridget's dad (grandfather to Billy) explained his experience. "I was pleased when my daughter said that Billy liked trains. I didn't know what *Thomas* was, but she explained that it was a television program that had talking trains. I didn't want to watch TV with Billy, but I asked if I could take him for a train ride when we came to visit, and my daughter thought it was a good idea. She has another baby at home, so she hadn't taken him for train rides yet. I used the Internet to plan a route that started near her house and ended by a McDonald's because she said his favorite food was french fries. We had a fine time, and my daughter had a couple of hours to visit with her mom and the baby."

Bridget took her dad's strong start and ran with it. "I took pictures of my dad and Billy when they set off that day. After my parents went home, we made a picture book with those photos plus some train pictures from the Web. Billy liked the book, and when he seemed to be losing interest in it, I put it away. The next time my parents were planning a visit, I brought the book out and told Billy he'd get to go on another train ride with Grandpa. On the next visit they went to McDonald's by train twice! Now Billy associates train rides with his grandpa and says 'Ride with Grandpa' whenever we see a real train. I hope they can go to new places in the future. For now, McDonald's is great!"

But what if parents report that a child's major interest is watching TV, or something even more narrow like ripping paper? Don't give up. There are still ways to indulge your grandchild in his pleasures, even if you don't fully understand them.

Andrea says, "My son Sam loves ripping boxes. When my folks came to town, I suggested that they take Sam to the grocery store and pick up a few things we needed, and I asked them to grab some empty cardboard boxes for him if they could. My mom totally surprised me by bringing home enough flattened boxes to last a month. She apparently made friends with the produce manager, and he took them both into the back of the store. My son will probably never forget the time he went 'behind' the supermarket with Grandma! I was amazed my mom could turn a boring supermarket trip into something completely fantastic for Sam."

Andrea recounted, "My son was all about the alphabet for a while. We had every alphabet puzzle you can imagine and all kinds of blocks and toys. When my parents came to town, I didn't have any good ideas about how they could use that to connect with him; actually I was tapped out. But it turned out that keeping it simple was best. My mom bought a set of fat magic markers and a pad of paper and wrote each letter on a different page. They looked at it together and then they added stickers to each page on a second pass. The third pass they used different colored markers. She understood that it was about repetition for him, so she didn't keep introducing new games; she stuck with the same thing the whole week. By the end of the visit, Nathan began to bring the pad and sit down next to her."

Starting Small

Outings or activities with grandparents or friends don't need to be big, memorable, or zany to be a success. In fact, starting small and building on success is a much better strategy than trying to make a huge impact with a trip to Disneyland. Find out what outings or activities already work well for this child. Does he have a favorite local park? Can you take him for a favorite snack, even if that means a fast-food restaurant? What if you brought him to his weekly swimming lesson and stayed to watch? Ask his parents what outings they take regularly and look for something that you can handle successfully. Keep in mind that for a child with autism, familiar and routine experiences tend to be more enjoyable than new and different settings that are potentially scary. Adding your presence to a familiar routine will make you a more familiar person. There must be places that this child is accustomed to visiting with his parents that you can replicate in your own style. If his parents agree, try to make at least one such trip during your visit. A successful visit to a familiar playground is a great start and an experience you can build on.

If there is more than one child in the family, consider taking each one on a separate outing instead of taking everyone together. In some families, group outings work well. But if you are unsure of your ability to handle a child with autism in a public place or of how to make a connection in the midst of excited sibling chatter, try to make the situation simpler.

All outings do not have to be equal in stature. For example, you may take a child with autism to a nearby playground and later take his sister to a special lunch in a restaurant. The key is to find ways to spend time with each child based on their interests and abilities.

If there are a few children in the family, you may find that there is a temptation to do one outing with the child who has autism and another for "everyone else." Resist that temptation. The message it sends to everyone is that your grandchild with autism is set apart, different, and cannot be included. You want to send the message instead that you value unique time with each child.

Some children with autism find restaurants monumentally difficult. They are loud, filled with a variety of smells, lots of talking, and tons of ambient language. The behavior expectations (things like sitting still, waiting patiently, and reacting appropriately to strangers asking questions) are very high, sometimes too high. If you are accustomed to planning outings around meals, or if you enjoy entertaining in restaurants, think carefully before placing that pressure on the family of a child with autism. At a minimum, ask your child if a restaurant is a possibility, and if he or she says it isn't, don't push. Instead ask what would be a better option. Bringing home a take-out meal or offering to help cook dinner at home may be a better way to handle mealtimes, and your outings can center around something other than food.

Bridging the Distance Between Visits

"When David was little, my mom came for a visit," Scott explains. "She tried to play with him, but he was always on the go, and she felt like she couldn't catch his attention for long. But David loved Dr. Seuss books, so she was able to read him his favorites. Before the end of her visit, we made a video of her reading his favorite book straight to the camera. What a hit! He watched that video again and again; it was one of his favorites. And the next time Grandma came for a visit, he ran to her the minute she walked in the door. She said the first line of the book to him in greeting, and it was like a private joke between them. It was magic."

This kind of project, where David's grandma found an interest that her grandson already had and used it to connect, was perfect. Finding that interest is the first step, and for a visiting grandparent it is critical. Once you've used it, memorialize it in video or in pictures for the time in between visits.

Photo albums, emails, and cards sent between visits can be a great way to maintain a connection, just as it is with all other children. But for a child with autism, try to send photos that reference the time you spent together or familiar places and things. Those will be the most successful at striking memory chords of a happy time together.

Go ahead and send greeting cards that tap into his particular interests. And when something works, don't feel shy about doing it again! Repetition is key to creating comfort for a child on the spectrum, and pleasures can actually be magnified when they are familiar in addition to being relevant. Perhaps with another child, sending a card with Elmo on it seems out of the question, completely outside your usual style. (Maybe you had never heard of Elmo until your last visit!) But for this child, make a tradition out of *always* sending a card with Elmo on it, at least until his parents can tell you that something else is "hot." Rather than wondering why Grandma always sends the same cards, your grandchild will begin to anticipate the fun tradition, and it will cue him to associate Elmo greeting cards with you. Most importantly, he'll remember your desire to understand and join in his interests.

Finding Holiday Happiness

Every year around the December holidays, friends and family struggle to choose the right gifts for a new generation of children who have access to a wide variety of technologies and toys.

But if you've taken the time to explore this child's interests in preparation for a visit, you are already ready for the gift-giving quandary. The important thing is always to select a gift with the recipient in mind. The touching thing about choosing a gift for a child with autism is that many of the usual evaluation metrics do not apply. He won't care how much money you spent, and it wouldn't occur to him to compare his gift to what someone else gave him, or what his sister got. He will simply appreciate it because it ties into an interest for him and because you gave it to him.

If your child has told you that your grandson loves going to his swimming lessons, send a brightly colored or personalized towel. If he loves a particular TV character, you can be confident that he'll love just about anything featuring that character.

If you can find a theme to repeat with variation at each holiday, that will serve you well for many years. Like sending Elmo greeting cards, inventing traditions and repeating them is a recipe for success. Isabel recalls, "I told my mom that my kids can never get enough Disney movies, so she goes to Target and asks the salesperson which movie is hot each year. The kids know that they'll get a new movie from Grandma every year, and they look forward to it. The DVDs are very easily wrapped and shipped, so it is great for everyone. And when she comes to visit, she can ask them how they liked it or even watch it with them."

"My parents travel a lot," says Kendra. "So every time they go somewhere, they buy a fun T-shirt for William. The other kids at school ask about his cool T-shirts, so they are a great social starter. It really doesn't matter where the T-shirt comes from, just adding a new one is fun! The only problem is parting with them when they get too small!"

In the end, it's showing that you are thinking of your grandchild that counts. The actual gift is much less important than the reminder that you love him.

Taking a Fallback Position

Finally, if you are hitting roadblocks or having trouble finding an interest that you can develop, fall back to finding ways to help the child's parents. Whether it is immediately apparent or not, having a child with autism can make for a complicated and sometimes difficult life. Ask if there are any errands you can run to help out. Don't tell the family what you want to do to help—ask what would be helpful.

Here are some things you can suggest:

- Can I bring dinner home as a take-out order from a favorite place?

- Can I do some grocery shopping?

- Does an adult need to stay home while therapists come to the house? I can serve in that capacity.

- Does your car need gas? I can take it over for a fill-up.

- Can I offer you my car to use for errands while you take yours in for a tune-up?

- Can I baby-sit, perhaps after the kids have fallen asleep so you can go out together, perhaps catch a movie?

It may be that connecting directly with the child must wait for a future visit. But every year you'll find that time and maturity have made a difference, and each visit offers a brand-new chance to connect. Keep trying!

Chapter 7

Taking the Show on the Road

· · · · ·

Remember the days when going out with a baby involved a diaper bag stuffed like a suitcase and the fortitude of a soldier setting out on a trek across the desert? Some things change and some things don't. When you have a child with autism, it may be that going out still looks like an organizational marvel.

But many desperate situations can be averted through preparation. So we'll start by looking at your tools and techniques to streamline. Truly intensive preparation need only happen a few times a year. From then on you can leverage and update as needed rather than starting over every time. Start with the vehicle you are driving. It is time to jettison ideas about image and revel in functionality.

Carmen remembers her first minivan. "My husband and I were in total agreement about this when we started a family. No minivan! An SUV felt more 'us.' So like a lot of parents in the nineties, we picked an SUV. It was rugged and fun, and we felt safe on the road. But when the SUV needed to be replaced, we looked at minivans because my sister raved about hers. Eventually we got one too. Since then we have laughed at ourselves a million times. Why did we hate the idea of a minivan so much? It is amazing and we take so many day and weekend trips now that we have it."

Minivans are like a multi-use room on wheels. Since the seats can be arranged in a variety of positions or removed completely, you can create different arrangements to suit everything from a carpool (all seats on board) to a trip to the beach (take out as many seats as possible at home and use the minivan as your changing room).

With a minivan you can be practically carefree about space when deciding what to take on road trips, since there is room enough to throw in whatever you need. Perhaps you'd like to grab that inflatable mattress you purchased as an indoor toy and throw it in too—you can pull over to accommodate a nap in the back.

Do you find yourself waiting when your children have therapy or lesson appointments? No problem. Instead of reading old magazines in a tired waiting room, crawl in the back, open up a book and relax in private. It is as comfortable as being on the couch at home. With a cell phone or a laptop, there is nothing you can't do from your minivan—otherwise known as your mobile office. Useless dead time becomes productive time.

And last but most certainly not least, the entertainment systems available in minivans are terrific. You may think that you are accustomed to the minor squabbling that goes along with road trips, but when it disappears in favor of happy and quiet viewing, it is a whole different feeling for the driver. Backseat bickering is a thing of the past. Even children with autism who genuinely like riding in cars may find the television makes longer trips more pleasurable. Movies or video games unite the backseat occupants into a happy audience instead of a captive group of passengers.

You may not be in a position to pick up a new minivan just for convenience's sake. But the next time an automobile discussion comes up in your household, consider it. Whether you buy a used Chevy or a fully loaded Honda, having a minivan can be life changing for a family with a child on the spectrum. More than any other vehicle, it is a family retreat on wheels. With it you know that you can always retire for a break in your driving "room," and you can bring along many of the comforts of home.

Tricking Out the Car You've Got

No matter your make and model, your car can be a refuge for the entire family. Keep a basic supply of necessities in your trunk or backseat so that you can always count on them. Find an inexpensive backpack or duffle that isn't in use and start with:

- A complete change of clothes (seasonally appropriate) for each child, including underwear for the potty trained

- Extra Pull-ups or diapers, moist wipes

- Packaged snacks that will stay fresh

- Water bottles and juice boxes

- Plastic bags for garbage, diaper disposal

- Small toy or treat, some kind of never-fail fidget or item of interest

- If you have a dog, a spare leash, a water bowl, a tennis ball, and one portion of food, just in case

Customize this starting list with your own must-have items. Whether it is a fresh book of Mad Libs, a Kidz Bop CD, a box of chocolate milk, a pacifier, or your child's favorite spoon, tailor these supplies to your child. Taking time to stock your car with a few crucial duplicates for a moment of need will pay off later.

The key to a successful car pack is to *always* replace what you use. There is nothing more frustrating than finding that you used up that perfect item the last time you got stressed and didn't replace it. If you've used something from the pack, bring the whole thing inside to refill as soon as you get home.

Remember that you may be eligible for special parking privileges. Visit your state's DMV website to get the correct form to apply for a blue placard. Many states accept autism spectrum disorder as a qualifying diagnosis for a blue parking pass (see chapter 1 for more information on this). When you are planning a day of fun, the last thing you want to do is waste good energy and effort on a large, crowded parking lot or a long walk to your destination. That walk can use up a good attitude because of the noise, odors, and effort required. If your child has behavioral difficulties or impulse control issues, a busy parking lot can be a hazard.

Keep Moving Forward

Like thumbprints, each child on the spectrum will have a unique combination of sensory issues and trouble spots. Time and experience go a long way for parents and kids in learning about the boundaries. Trial and error is the best way to find out what works and what doesn't. As time goes by, kids with autism spectrum disorders learn to cope with more and to process a greater variety of sensory information. These are both reasons that you often hear parents say, "It gets better as they get older."

Placement Matters

If you have a child who is interested in spatial distance and directions, you may find that sitting in the backseat unable to see the road ahead creates a sense of frustration and agitation in your child.

Katherine explains, "When my son was three, we were heading home from his school. When I approached our regular turnoff, the turn lane had been blocked and a detour was marked. I didn't think anything of it; I just drove by the usual turn knowing there was an alternate way home in another couple of blocks. But in the backseat Aaron went ballistic! Until that day I had no idea that he was watching every move we made, every street we turned on. He knew our surroundings with incredible detail. I learned that when he could see the road ahead he became infinitely calmer in the car. It was an epiphany."

Every parent is instructed early that all children must be strapped into age-appropriate car seats and are not allowed in the front seat until they are twelve. But what is not discussed is that there can be exceptions. Does your child try to unstrap his seat belt when he is in the backseat? Is he struggling to see out the front window? Does he frequently cry or need your attention while you are driving? If you find that you are twisting around or frequently pulling over to manage, the entire family may be in danger. Sitting in the front seat may make a substantial difference in your child's safety (and your family's ability to enjoy outings). If this is the case, you can apply to the National Transportation Safety Board (NTSB) for just such an exception. Applicants must write a letter that explains why their child is less safe in the backseat than in the front. If the NTSB approves, they will send you a return letter to keep in your glove compartment. In the event of a traffic stop, the letter will suffice to explain that your child has permission to ride in the front seat. If you'd like to write such a letter, direct it to the NTSB at 490 L'Enfant Plaza, SW, Washington, DC 20594.

You're the Deejay

Playing music in the car may seem obligatory to you, but there's a chance that it is draining some of your child's ability to cope before you arrive at your destination. You need to know if that is the case in order to plan effectively. Most kids on the spectrum tend to be deeply affected by sound. The impact can be positive or negative, or it can vary depending on the circumstances. Any sound that comes through the car speakers needs to be considered. For example, if you routinely play the radio, what you think of as music may be interspersed with booming voices and grab-your-attention advertisements that you've learned to tune out. For the same reason, talk radio may be more annoying to your child than you have imagined. Learning where your child's auditory limits lie takes time and careful observation. But the car is a great place to do it, and it can be a fun exploration.

You'll need to experiment to find the best amount of input. Play some favorite music in the car for a week, and then do a week of radio silence. After the first week, consider how your outings have gone in general. Try to take some brief notes on the general outcome of both small, routine errands as well as any larger outings or unfamiliar destinations. Then do the same kind of assessment after a week of silence and compare. Don't do this kind of evaluation on a day-by-day basis, because there are too many things that might affect each individual outing. A certain mood on a particular day, rain, or some other seemingly irrelevant factor may be having an impact without you knowing it. But stretched out over a week you'll find that you can review a general picture without any one day dictating the outcome.

If you compare your weeks side by side and find that the week when the radio was on was filled with crankiness, difficulty transitioning when it was time to get out of the car, lower levels of cooperation or unwillingness to enter destinations or participate once there, you may have discovered that the radio or music in the car is having a negative impact on your child. You can experiment still further with different kinds of music, simpler, less-frenetic styles, or singing yourself to see if you can eliminate or reduce what is difficult. Each time you make a change, try it for a few days unless the immediate reaction is so negative that your answer is obvious.

If you do come to the conclusion that music in the car reduces your child's ability to cope at your destination, you may have to give it a rest. You can reintroduce it in small doses over time to build up an ability to enjoy it. Most importantly, know the boundaries and you can control the effect.

Even if they enjoy music in the car, some kids get edgy because they find that they want to control the dials. That sets up a different challenge, still one you'll need to address.

Dani explained, "Levi has always loved controls—on CD players, TVs, everything electronic. We enjoyed having music in the car for a while, but then we found he was getting antsy because he wanted to control the buttons. When it started he gave us his instructions, saying stuff like 'new song' or 'change station.' We thought it was a good language opportunity, and we wanted to reward the speech, so we did it. But it was a trap! It got unpleasant pretty quickly."

She continues, "We tried turning the music off but that didn't work. He would unbuckle himself and try to reach over the front seat to turn it back on! It scared me to death. Thank goodness for MP3 players. We got him one for his birthday and loaded it up with favorites. Now he has headphones in the backseat, and we can even keep the radio on the front speakers for us. Everyone is happy. And Levi can change the song as often as he likes!"

If you decide to give an MP3 player to your child, consider adding the additional expense of a protective case. You can expect any small device to take a beating at the hands of a child, but especially with a child who has autism. A protected MP3 player also opens up new opportunities for fun in unexpected places. If your child enjoys swimming, you may discover a big thrill when you can bring music along! Check out OtterBox, a company that makes absolutely waterproof cases. On the practical side, waterproof MP3 players can also help keep out the noise at indoor pools, which is a serious deterrent to many kids with autism. An iPod contained in an OtterBox can totally change the experience. Go to otterbox.com to see their selection. And you can really save money by choosing a refurbished iPod on eBay that matches up with a clearance model OtterBox. Last season's models can be up to 75 percent off!

Video Entertainment in the Car

Depending on whom you ask, having a television in the car is either a sign of the fall of western civilization or a gift from heaven. For many parents, it is a godsend. If your car is regularly home to bickering, boredom, and inter-sibling stress, a trip to a local electronics store for a portable model may be your relief.

Some vehicles come with built-in TV systems. Or you can purchase a separate system that can be strapped to the back of a front seat for rear-seat viewing. As mentioned earlier, car television can be terrific, and there are advantages to either kind of system, but generally the built-in systems are best for children with autism. They have centralized controls that are managed by the front-seat occupants, and the sound is transmitted over the vehicle's built-in speakers.

When you use a portable player, the controls are right on the unit and available to the children watching. And the sound tends to require headphones for adequate volume, and not all kids can tolerate those.

Marina says, "When we got a minivan with a built-in TV, it literally changed our lives. It sounds so ridiculous, but it opened up so many options. Our kids became happier in the car than they had ever been! Now we can take much longer trips, and we are willing to try things further away. If Noah needs to stay in the car while some of us do things that he doesn't like, that works too. I wouldn't trade that car TV for the most exciting sports car in the world!"

Some may suggest that children with car TVs miss out on looking out the window. But if everyone enjoys the trips more, it might be a choice between fun, new experiences and not going at all. Adventures with family should always win in that choice!

When it comes to choosing what to watch on the car system, try to include everyone to some degree. The wider the age span of your passengers, the more challenging this can become. But many animated shows include aspects to please a wide variety of viewers, so those are a good choice. And Gerald says, "When we got our minivan with a DVD player, the first thing I bought was a season of *The Muppet Show* on DVD. Our son who has autism loves *Sesame*

Street, so he took to the Muppets right away. And my older kids liked it too. From the front seat my wife and I get quite a few laughs listening to the jokes that the kids don't quite get!"

Fun in the car isn't limited to TVs. Here are some other car toys that your child may enjoy:

- Handheld "fidgets"—kush balls, squeezy stress balls, Thera-Bands, a collection of textured fabric samples, Theraputty

- Animals—rubber reptiles, plastic zoo and farm animals, small stuffed animals

- Nintendo DS or other handheld electronic games— These can be costly, but if your child does enjoy them, they are both single and multi-user aspects. And they can be a point of connection for your child with other kids, since many others have them and enjoy talking about them. They can share cartridges, talk about games, and even interact through the game machines in some cases. Parents need to consider their personal electronic threshold with this decision. Some think these games allow too much technology into our kids' lives, while others value the enjoyment they provide. There is a fine-motor component to their use in addition to the interactive aspects. You can start some research online at the Edutaining Kids website: www.edutainingkids.com/videogames.html.

Getting There Can Be Half the Fun

Consider the ride to your destination part of the fun. Sure there are going to be times when the driver needs to focus on the road, when adults in the front seat want to talk, or when silence is golden, but try to take your mind off the GPS occasionally to check in and share a rearview mirror smile, game, or sing-along. For kids who love the feeling of motion, time in the car can be their favorite time of the day. They may be more receptive to interaction there than at home. Don't miss out on being a part of it.

Chapter 8

Regular Life and Weekends

· · · · ·

As fun and exciting as big-ticket family adventures can be, you also need to balance that stimulation with a certain amount of predictability. The truth is that all kids love and depend on routines for feelings of safety and strength. As much as they enjoy going on wild outings and discovering new places, a solid base of fun that can be anticipated and revisited is important in developing the skills for the higher-level excitement and thrill seeking.

Those events and outings that repeat regularly don't have to be boring. There's no need to confuse routine and consistency with dullness. Regular outings can be spicy and fun and contain spontaneity too, as long as they are built on a foundation where the kids feel safe and protected from unpleasant surprises.

Most parents are familiar with the usual playgroup scene. Groups of parents (or caregivers) meet at alternating houses and hang out while the kids play. But many autism moms have truly terrible memories of these playgroups as being the source of their first worries and the place where they first realized their child was different.

Melanie recalls, "I looked forward to going to this playgroup with a group of women I really liked. But then I'd spend the whole time chasing Matthew and trying to keep him from breaking things or getting into trouble. At some point I woke up to the fact that all my friends were sitting around talking, eating, hanging out, and I was frantically watching every move my son made as he grabbed for knick-knacks on shelves, cried about the noise, and melted down with a total inability to cope. I finally looked around and asked myself, why is everyone having a good time except me? Pretty soon I made the first doctor's appointment, and the rest is history."

If you have these kinds of memories of toddler play-groups, it's time to put them behind you. Now that you are informed about autism and your child, you know why those events didn't work. And you know more about planning situations that have a better chance to work. You can create a better basis for a get-together that involves other kids and other parents without repeating the mistakes that were only due to lack of knowledge.

Make contact with a few other parents whose kids have special needs. Try setting up a regularly scheduled come-if-you-can playdate that happens every week at the same time without a lot of planning. Pick a favorite park, and tell everyone you'll be there Sundays around 11 am. Spread the word as widely as possible and recruit friends. It is important to make it a habit to go on a regular basis as often as you can. This way your children will become accustomed to the routine week after week, and other people's kids will too. That will lead to comfort and a decrease in the amount of care and attention they require. The siblings of special needs kids can get to know each other in a casual playground context and develop relationships that will help them over time when they face more sophisticated issues.

When you are developing a standing weekly playgroup, there are some important logistical aspects to consider in order to create the best chance for success. The first is location. It is critical to pick a place where you won't be surrounded by crowds of typical kids and their care-givers, so the favorite local playground is not necessarily the first choice here. In those kinds of places, too much time gets devoted to watching for inappropriate behavior and repairing missteps, not to mention polite chitchat with strangers. It is counterproductive to the idea of relaxing with other special needs families.

Look for a school that will allow you to use their playground during non-school hours or a park off the beaten track. The more enclosed the location is the better. Everyone needs to feel reasonably secure letting the kids play freely, not to mention letting behaviors fly in an environment where no one will have to shush or apologize. Of course parents have to keep their usual watchful eye on safety and particularly look out for anger bursts. And each parent will have to decide for themselves how much to take advantage of "teachable moments." There is a temptation to see this kind of a playgroup as an educational setting where social skills can be worked on. But as much as possible, let the time unfold without a lot of heavy intervention or facilitation. Playgroup time isn't therapy time, it's fun time. More than anything, it is critical that your child enjoys it as much as possible so that your family can return week after week.

Consider the scheduling. Work with a core group of families that have shown an interest in getting together to find a mutually workable time. If you want to make it a primary caregiver playgroup, a weekday time will work, but a regular weekend time turns it into a family event and that may be preferable. Everyone needs chances to unwind and connect, and most special needs families find the weekends a time of much less therapy and more free time. Often the working parent misses out on connections made during a week of interacting with caregivers and therapists and sitting in waiting rooms. A weekend schedule will allow the alternate parent to come as well. Two big issues to consider when scheduling over the weekend are religious obser- vances (avoid the times families are commonly at worship if that is a big factor in your community) and sports. As kids get older (siblings and special needs kids alike), things like soccer and baseball games are scheduled at common times. Avoiding those will help promote attendance.

If you find a location that is near a school or public building, investigate the bathroom facilities and if neces- sary, inquire about access for your families. A weekly play- group can be a lot easier with a bathroom nearby. If a key is needed, your core families can take turns being the key master, or one family that makes a habit of coming can be the holder.

Spread the word about your playgroup. Start with a handful of friends who are committed to showing up every week. But as time goes on, cast a wider net. There are lots of families out there coping with similar circumstances these days, and connecting with them and sharing lessons learned can be a great way to shortcut difficulties, not to mention create lasting friendships. Especially as more and more kids enter the special education system and funding sources become increasingly meager, parents working together can be a tremendous source of community support. If you can invite and welcome more families from your area, you'll be strengthening your network even as you widen your children's world. Be sure to tell everyone to bring their own snacks, a blanket to sit on, and any toys that will make the time fun for their kids.

Here are some not-too-taxing ways to spread the word about your playgroup:

- Post about it in your local online group. ("Please Join Us for a Playgroup for Families of Special Needs Kids! We get together at Jefferson Park every Sunday at 2 p.m. Bring the whole family and join us. We gather by the water fountain!") Some groups try to wear red T-shirts to be recognizable to each other, others locate an out-of-the-way meeting spot where they tend to be the only ones there. An elementary school playground on the weekend can be a terrific spot. You may even be able to talk the school principal into letting your group keep a copy of the bathroom key.

- Put a note up in the offices of local service providers and other special needs magnet locations. Speech therapists, occupational therapists, and psychologists all tend to have waiting rooms. The local swimming pool and skating rink are well used by special needs families looking for fun ways to spend time. Look for bulletin boards or ask the provider if you can post a note.

- Craigslist (www.craigslist.org) has online bulletin boards in an ever-increasing list of cities and states. Posting in the Community section is free.

- Send a message to local parent groups or mothers' clubs, churches, or synagogues.

- Ask at your child's school if they can include a notice in their communications.

- Use a website like Vista Print (www.vistaprint.com) to get free business cards made with the details of your playgroup. Then you can share them or post them easily.

You don't have to go crazy or turn grassroots marketing into your career. But if you and a core group of friends carry a few copies of a notice in your purses or pockets, you can put them up around town as opportunities present themselves. There are huge benefits to interacting with families whose children are at different stages of development, even more than in the world of typical children. Other parents may have seen more and learned different lessons. They can help you even as you help them.

Get That Feeling of Festival

Once established, weekly playgroups don't have to be static. You can use holidays, events, and the weather to develop ideas for additional fun. If you don't have a means of communication in place (such as a Yahoo Group where the members all belong), you may need to collect email addresses so you can spread the word about events. Different families can take turns planning and announcing events. Megan says, "I don't know how it happened because I was never a party-planning type before. But now I get into it. I used to try to get other people to step up, but it didn't really work, and I hated that effort. So I do it because I enjoy it and so do my kids. If other families enjoy it too, so much the better!"

Here are some great ideas for playgroup fun:

- *Puddle stomping day.* Don't stay inside at the first sign of rainy weather. Advertise the first rainy playgroup of autumn as your Puddle Stomper. Suggest everyone wear rubber boots and bring umbrellas, towels, and a change of clothes. Let the kids go crazy, get wet, take their shoes off, whatever feels good! Water dries and mud washes off.

- *Mardi Gras* (in February or March) is always a fun excuse for a party. Mardi Gras beads are a huge hit with kids, as are funny hats, masks, Zydeco, and dancing. Making your own masks and fun food can spark up a dull time of year.

- *Slipping and sliding.* If your location permits, you can hook up a hose and have a warm weather playgroup. Everyone can bring his or her favorite water toys. Slip 'n Slides are tremendous fun, and water guns and even a plain-vanilla sprinkler can create big fun on a hot day. Be sure to tell people to bring dry clothes and a towel.

- *Bounce house.* If everyone chips in, the cost of a bounce house rental can be pretty reasonable. They range from fancy and more expensive to simple bounce houses, and they are rented usually by the day. Often at public events where a bounce house is part of the scene, our kids get squeezed out by other kids or their behavior attracts attention. Having one at your private playgroup for special needs families will help all the kids become better accustomed to them, and no one will mind if your child wants to lie down in the corner and feel everyone else jumping around him. One person will need to handle the collection of money, but another can make the reservation and logistical arrangements to distribute the effort required. The money collection can be handled in advance at a playgroup, or if someone is willing to foot the bill, people can pay for admittance (see chapter 2 for more information).

- *Ride 'em out.* If your playgroup location has a paved area, have a ride-on day! Everyone can bring their favorite wheels, from tricycles, wagons, and scooters to strollers or skates. This is a fun chance for siblings to show off their skills while their brother or sister gets extra help from parents. And for those kids who have not yet developed an interest in ride-on toys, the exposure to what other kids are doing and how much fun it is will be a great lead-in to that concept.

- *Mother's Day.* Some families have their own traditions for Mother's Day. But you can schedule a Mother's Day playgroup either on the holiday or at a separate time. Any day can be Mother's Day! Bring lawn chairs for moms to lounge on regally while dads and partners supervise an art project of easy-to-assemble crowns for the Queens for a Day. The crown is an easy outdoor art project that can be as simple or elaborate as the child wants, and if art is not "their thing," then that's fine too. There's an easy set of instructions for a crown art project at http://crafts.kaboose.com/king-for-a-day.html. Think tin foil!

- *Father's Day.* Don't forget Dad. Get the lawn chairs out again for another regal relaxation day, or do something different like bringing a plastic golf game, lawn bowling, or croquet.

- *Bang those drums.* Ask everyone to bring a musical instrument of any kind. It can be a hand drum, tambourine, kitchen tools, or maracas. You can have the kids make their own instruments too, with Tupperware or empty cartons partially filled with gravel. If you have a musically inclined family in the group, see if they can bring extra instruments for kids who didn't bring anything or want to try something new. It will help to have a boom box playing some Caribbean or African music, and everyone can play along!

- *Costume day.* Your playgroups can have themes, like Be a Pirate Day, Dress Like a Sports Star, Hippie Day, or Hat Day. Keep the themes simple so that parents can grab items from around the house, and kids with sensory issues can either keep it simple or opt out. Anyone with a collection can bring extras for kids to share.

- *Rocket man.* There are some great rocket toys available that range from the simple and super-safe to the more exciting. You can usually find a variety of rockets at a

toy store or online at Amazon under Toys and Games ›
Rockets. Our Rocket playgroups have been some of the
best on record, with parents setting off the more complicated rockets for the enjoyment of the crowd, and kids
using stomp rockets (Styrofoam projectiles set on small
air pumps, which the child steps on to create the rocket
launch) and other easy rocket toys, like those relying on
water pressure for power. Wait until you see how much
all kids love a loud group countdown with a big whoosh
at the end and lots of applause! Magic.

As fun as the rocket playgroup can be, it does require
some extra thought to safety. Any rockets that require more
than stomping power to launch should only be handled by
an adult, and only in an area where there is no possibility
that a person could be hurt by a projectile or "astronaut"
falling to earth. We're talking about play rockets sold at toy
stores, not M-80s or anything explosive! Nothing with fire-
power is needed. The excitement is in the anticipation and
the event, not to mention watching parents get out and have
a "blast" right beside the kids.

Don't worry if your child doesn't fully participate or
stays on the perimeter of the gathering. It may take time
for him to get accustomed to the event, or the activities
may not grab his interest. But you'll find that over time,

his participation will increase. Watching other kids play and participate is the best encouragement.

Take lots of photos of everyone involved and share them afterwards to help bring the community together, especially on the special event days. The photos can also be used by kids to learn the names of their friends, create storybooks of weekend events to share at school, or prepare for future events. Absolutely everyone loves to see photos of recent fun. Try to arrange for at least one person to bring a camera, and the more the merrier. There are online sites devoted to photo sharing like Snapfish and Kodakgallery.com, but if you are using Yahoo or Google groups to manage your contact list, this is another time when it will be a big help in developing your community. These sites have a section for posting pictures right in the online application, and once they have been uploaded, it is an easy step to email the group and let them know they are online.

Other Ways to Create Routine Fun

Kids can find weekends a total departure from the routine feeling they associate with weekdays. Whether the weekdays are filled with a group program, day care, school, or individual therapy, it tends to be busy time and regimented, predictable all the way until bedtime. When the weekend arrives, the reliable routine disappears abruptly, and a lifestyle full of choices and changes kicks in. Making it less free-form, with predictable placeholders, will calm the chaos.

Try to maintain some set points in your weekend schedule for your child to anticipate. If swimming is a big interest, find the times available at a local pool and go every week. If bowling is a favorite activity, make a ritual of going at the same favorite time. Anything errand-like that you need to do regularly can become an event, like a weekly trip with Dad to the big-box store, or a visit to the pet shop to look at the tropical fish and buy dog food. An event is whatever you call an event. If a place of worship is a part of your lives, you already know it is a great schedule anchor. The need for everyone to be ready to leave together, dressed, and set to go, makes it a bonding experience just as the service itself is. As your kids develop the understanding that weekends operate on a rhythm of their own, which is predictable and within their ability to handle, they'll look forward to it more and more. The meltdowns and over-stimulation signs will cool, and families will see less and less of the situations that cause stress for everyone.

Last but not least, remember that splitting up into family subgroups is not only okay but sometimes best for everyone. It is not something to feel badly about or to avoid at all costs. Andrea explains, "We learned the hard way that Jimmy couldn't handle the gymnasium during my daughter's volleyball games. It was too loud, and there was nothing of interest for him there. Instead of having family time, the reality was that my husband and I were taking turns taking him outside while the other watched the game. We finally decided that we had to split up. But it worked out really well. My husband started taking Jimmy to the big-box store every week where he loves to ride in the huge cart and sample foods. It became their special thing, and it is practical too, so they felt a sense of accomplishment. And I really enjoy the volleyball games now, much more since I'm not worrying about Jimmy. We go out with the team for pizza afterwards, which we used to avoid. No one lost out, and I wish I hadn't worried about it so much."

Individual time with each of your kids is important, and for each child it is special. It recharges your batteries and theirs. But like many aspects of life with a child on the spectrum, it can be a matter of finding balance. Andrea continues, "Once we got more accustomed to doing stuff apart, we discovered that we have a tendency to swing like a pendulum. Sometimes we'll realize that we are doing too many things apart, and we aren't making time to be together. It begins to feel like Jimmy is 'mine' and Carolyn is 'Bill's.' I never want that to feel like the norm; it should only be temporary. But other times we'll discover that things are feeling wrong because we are trying to do everything together, and we've lost the joy. So we have to constantly consider our plans and balance things out. Neither way—always together or always divided—works all the time. We're happiest when we get in balance. It's a moving target, but we are always trying."

Chapter 9

Enjoying the Wider World

· · · · ·

Fortunately, parents aren't the only ones who have discovered that kids with special needs often have a unique sense of fun and enjoy adventure. There is a segment of the professional community that understands how tremendously important motivation and enjoyment are to learning, and they've developed exciting new ways to use the activities that interest our kids as learning tools. These translate into huge opportunities for you and your family! As parents we have to lead our kids to these special opportunities and help them be comfortable enough to explore and benefit from them. Later the activities themselves can become opportunities for family fun or regular therapeutic approaches.

Delving into Your Home's Natural Resources

No matter where you live, the natural landscape is bound to offer a variety of potential activities. If you are near a coastline, the beach is a huge feature. Whether you are going into the waves to body surf or boogie board, collecting shells, or building sand castles, a day at the beach is a pleasure for everyone.

Steve and his children have developed a unique tradition of creating huge sand castles with tunnels. They bring a variety of shovels in different shapes and tennis balls, which they roll through the tunnels of their ever-more-elaborate constructions. "It started out small," he says, "but became so much fun. Now every time we go to the beach we try to top our last construction and make something cooler. Right before we leave we take a quick photo using my phone so we can keep a scrapbook!"

Mountains and hiking can be terrific, and miles of flat terrain are great for biking. Are you near a lake? Boating is a terrific experience with huge sensory benefits. Think about what your area offers that you can explore and how you can adapt the usual tourist destinations to work for your family. Since you live nearby, you have an advantage that the usual tourist lacks: flexibility. You can try the same destination more than once, you can develop a routine that works, and you can repeat it when it does. Take advantage of this opportunity to make local attractions more fun for you than the average visitor.

"There is a statue in town of a Civil War general," Clark says. "It doesn't offer much, on its face. But we started making it a game to bring different things to put in his outstretched hands and take a picture. For a while we brought something different every week, like a flower, or a kite. It turned into a joke, and we would run around the house looking for funny things to give him and then take a picture. Our favorite was the time we put a shower cap on his head and a back scrubber in his hand and took a picture of him with my twins, who were wrapped in towels. It may be a little silly, but we have a great photo collection!"

Don't forget to check out the tourist attractions in your area. Residents often forget these attractions, becoming accustomed to their presence without taking advantage of their fun. Don't let that happen. No matter where you live, pretend you are coming to town for the first time and see what your place has to offer. Ask yourself what you would do if out-of-town guests came to visit. Become your own guest and explore those things for yourself.

Giddy up! Getting on Horseback

There are several different styles of horseback riding available for special needs kids, and what you can find in your area may dictate your choice. Here are some of the options:

Hippotherapy, a therapeutic horseback riding program, is performed by a certified physical therapist or occupational therapist, often with a doctor's recommendation or prescription. Generally the providers are certified in hippotherapy in addition to certification in their field, so insurance may cover a portion of the cost. If your child has specific gross motor goals or needs to work on muscle development, hippotherapy may be a good fit.

A hippotherapy session is often attended by four adults: the certified therapist, a horse handler, and two side walkers to guarantee stability and safety for the child. The number of side walkers may be reduced as the child gains confidence and the provider gets to know the student. Slow and steady riding in a closed arena is interspersed with games (things like tossing a bean bag through a hoop) or reaching tasks ("grab that puppet on top of the post!") to encourage the child to use his body in accordance with specific goals.

An alternative to hippotherapy is a therapeutic riding program, which can also be described as horseback riding lessons for kids with special needs. These providers are usually not certified in occupational therapy or physical therapy, but instead focus on creating a safe program dedicated to developing riding proficiency and confidence. The movements a child performs are less intense, and goals are focused on riding proficiency, horse care, and interaction and enjoyment as opposed to increasing physical challenges and body movement.

If you are considering a riding program for your child, be sure to visit on your own first, ideally at a time when lessons are in progress. Some questions to consider:

- Are the instructors and staff friendly and encouraging?

- If teenage volunteers are participating in the program, how much education do they get about autism and interacting with our kids?

- Do the students seem happy and confident?

- Ask questions about how they work through fear, disinclination, or downright resistance on the part of new students. Some teachers use games, sensory exploration, and play on horseback to encourage engagement and create fun. Other programs may be more focused on developing riding skills (such as learning to start, stop, and sit properly on the horse). A combination of these approaches is great.

Billy's mom Heather says, "When we first started going to the program, my son seemed afraid and was totally unwilling. Friends had told me that their kids really liked it, so I was disappointed. But our instructor didn't want us to give up. She said lots of kids feel that way at first. She didn't push Billy too hard, but she did move him out of his comfort zone little by little. They did some lessons sitting astride barrels, and they spent time brushing and touching the horse. She was great about using language he could understand and giving him time to adjust. When Billy got on a horse for the first time, he was scared. They had him bring his chewing toy with him. But when the horse started walking, he lit up. Now his riding lesson is the highlight of his week. And I volunteer for the program and help with fund-raising!"

For safety reasons, your child will need to wear some kind of helmet while riding. If he has a bike helmet he's used to, you may want to ask if he can wear it while riding. Some programs require students to wear special helmets designed for the sport. If that is the case, get a sense of how heavy they are and in what condition. Sometimes kids with sensory issues will reject a helmet that is very worn or dirty without trying it on. The program may be willing to loan you one before your first lesson so you can practice wearing it at home. That will make it a little more familiar.

One last tip: If you have been watching your child's riding lessons for a time and feel disconnected from his experience, ask the program coordinator if you can share a lesson with your son. You may be able to go on a trail ride together, or participate in a parent-child riding event some weekend if the program is willing to hold one. Many providers become so focused on teaching the kids and maximizing their experience, they may not realize parents want to be part of it and connect with their children at the same time. Some programs allow parents to work as side walkers, but that can be a distraction to a child, so it's not usually recommended. You could also volunteer behind the scenes. But if your child is comfortable on horseback and you'd like to make it more of a family experience, give it a try. Your child may enjoy being the "expert" and he'll see you in a whole new way!

There are a great many books, videos, and toys related to horseback riding. Seek out these resources to help introduce ideas and increase comfort. From videos to coloring books, stories to toy horses, they will help your child become familiar with horses and the words we use about them. And if your local supermarket or car wash has one of those ride-on horses that rock for a coin, give it a try!

Find the Nearest Body of Water

Most kids love water, and kids with autism tend to love it even more. The sooner you are able to expose your child to water and develop water-safety skills, the easier it will be to find more fun opportunities in the future. So the time to start is now. Check out a local pool and invest in some swimming lessons to help your child gain confidence and develop a lifelong love of the water. Even in winter, there are often warm-water indoor pools to be found at community centers or even hotels. If your child loves the bathtub, start looking around now so you have bigger and better places to swim before it becomes a tight fit.

Being in or on the water feeds our kids' need for motion and rhythm beautifully. Look in your area for bodies of water that offer recreation. You might be near the ocean, a lake, a man-made fishing pond, or a reservoir, but whatever the style, you can be sure that people will be finding ways to enjoy it, and it is a great opportunity for your family to share a fun activity together.

Boating and More

Boats or water crafts of any kind are tremendous sensory experiences for children. And the required safety equipment tends to be manageable (things like flotation vests, rubber-soled shoes, etc.). The payoff runs the gamut from gentle rocking motion to an exciting, choppy, spray-filled ride.

If you live near a lake, explore activities such as paddle boating, rowboating, and kayaking. You may need to invest serious effort to propel your child into breezes and motion on the water, but with time you may be able to convince your child to take a more active role, leading to some "heavy work" activity that puts their muscles into action too. Rafting, canoeing, and kayaking are also pursuits that could lead to a fun family camping trip.

A Word or Two about the Beach

While tremendously exciting, the noise, the smell, and the sensations of the beach can be potentially overwhelming to a child with autism. If you have a child on the spectrum, be prepared for the possibility that enjoying a day at the beach is something that can take time, practice, and some effort. You may need to work up to it, starting with an hour or two out and moving the bar higher with each visit.

"We went to the beach for the first time when my son was two," Kellie remembers. "We didn't know about autism yet. But I'll never forget that day. He was completely overwhelmed, and he became frenzied. We were very surprised. He wanted to run and run and run. When we tried to turn around and head back to our blanket, he cried and screamed. My vision of sitting on a blanket while he played in the sand was smashed. My husband and I were completely exhausted and eventually we had to carry him, still screaming, to the car. Anyone watching us would have been horrified. I was horrified!

"But when we recovered, we tried again. We kept going back, but we would go for shorter periods of time. Before long, the place began to make sense to Chase. It took time, and we still have to watch carefully to make sure he doesn't get too far from us, but the beach has become his favorite place in the world. He loves to stand hip-deep in the water and feel the waves. And when we say it is time to go, he even helps me carry things to the car. There was a time when I couldn't even imagine that. I am glad we stuck with it. It paid off!"

The sight of the endless horizon, the sensation of sand under the feet and as far as the eye can see, the crashing of the waves and the smell of the salt can induce reactions that range from fear to excitement to withdrawal. The first time you go to the beach, be cautious and expect the unexpected. Here are a few tips:

- Find a beach that allows you to park near the sand, so your vehicle is available as a retreat and also a place to keep more than you want to carry.

- Try not to bring too much down to the beach with you. Leave things in the car and bring only essentials to the sand. You don't want to be loaded down with stuff and unable to chase your child if he bolts.

- Don't bring your dog to the beach until you know you can handle your child and your dog safely there.

- If you are going as a family, consider buying some inexpensive walkie-talkies. They work well on the beach (cell phones may not work or can get damaged). Walkie-talkies will keep your family in touch when you split up, and they are great fun for kids to play with too.

- Use swim shirts (also known as rash guards) routinely. If you always put one on your child, he will come to expect it. They will translate into less application of sunblock and more freedom for your child. Always choose bright colors to make your child most recognizable on the beach or in public pools. If your child wears a wetsuit on the beach, you can put a bright rashguard on top to distinguish him from the black-clad crowd. If he will tolerate a hat, that will also be a big help in sun protection. But if he won't, do your best with a high-SPF, odorless lotion on the face and legs. Don't chase your child all day with a hat; you'll just be adding to everyone's stress (and odds are good that the hat will get lost in the bargain).

The first few visits to the beach may not yield father-son Frisbee games or a relaxing read of the latest bestseller. But time and repetition will help your child adjust to the overwhelming sensations and get regulated and organized. The beach may turn out to be one of your most powerful destinations once you conquer the fear or intense fight-or-flight reaction it can inspire.

Everybody's Gone Surfing

Over the last few years, several organizations have sprung up to help get kids with autism on surfboards. This comes from a growing understanding of the power behind the experience. These dedicated groups use skilled volunteers and apply incredible energy to make surfing available to as many special needs children as possible. Check the Appendix or search the Internet for organizations serving your area. It may be that none operate where you live, but keep surfing in the back of your mind in case the day comes when you're planning a vacation on the coast or an island.

Surfing often requires that your child wear a wetsuit. Because of the length of time they'll spend in the water, it makes sense to eliminate cold as a problem as much as possible. Programs that have kids wearing wetsuits will usually provide suits in the right size for the day. However, putting on and wearing a wetsuit can be intense sensations. But some kids who like the feeling of pressure and tightness will really like the suit once they are in it!

Wetsuits are probably heavier than any clothes your child has ever worn, even cold weather gear. They fit very tightly and cover the entire body (except feet and hands) and zip up in the back. Getting in it involves wriggling and tugging. You may want to talk to your child about the wetsuit in advance or share a Social Story about the process of putting it on and taking it off. (Taking it off means allowing it to turn completely inside out as it peels away.) You can talk about why he'll be wearing it and the benefits to having an extra skin. Use photographs of experienced surfers in action to show the suits, because there is ample evidence that surfers are cool, have fun, and look sharp out on the ocean! You'll find great pictures in surfing magazines to make a collage, or with Google Images on the Web. YouTube also has some exciting images of surfers having fun. Your library or local bookstore should also have books about surfing. Here are some to look for that come in at different levels:

- *Kimo's Surfing Lesson* by Kerry Germain and Nicolette Moore

- *Rhinos Who Surf* by Julie Mammano

- *My Surf Lesson: Look Before You Leap* by Roberto Diaz and David Carles

- *S Went Surfing* by Ruth Moen Cabanting

- *Ocean in Motion! Surfing and the Science of Waves* by Paul Mason

If the surfing isn't a hit or the wetsuit is a hurdle, there are plenty of other terrific ways to enjoy the ocean. You can do other activities and perhaps try again later. Some kids would prefer to play in the sand, and building sand castles close to the surf can open the door to lessons in tides and astronomy, not to mention a way to be close to the mighty ocean without taking big risks.

Other Ocean Options

Boogie boards are lightweight, short, and easy-to-manage foam plastic boards for riding small waves close to shore. They're a terrific gateway to surfing as well as a ton of fun in their own right. They can be found at a wide variety of price ranges at sporting goods stores or through online vendors, but strong and sturdy specimens are available for around $30.

Body surfing is a way for strong swimmers to feel the power of the waves without an accessory. And even young children can get a thrill by lying facedown in shallow surf and letting the waves carry them farther in to shore. Jumping the waves is a hugely fun activity available to all kids, from the confident to the newbies. Learning to get wet, overcome fear, and enjoy the ocean is a wonderful way to spend some time.

One thing that a parent can never forget at the beach is safety. Never rely on public lifeguards to do the work of constant vigilance with your kids around the water. They not only have to be watching a lot of people all at once, but they also may have no understanding or awareness of autism. Even strong swimmers who are accustomed to swimming in pools will not be used to unique conditions like undertows or uneven ground and a variety of different conditions that can arise on shore. Always watch your own children carefully and put your beach novel aside. If your child is not a strong swimmer, look at flotation vests at sporting goods or variety stores. They are lightweight and non-constricting. They'll add a huge measure of safety. Children should never be left unattended around the water, no matter how great their ability.

Keep in mind also that at the beach there is little in the way of boundaries. Some kids get a full blast of wide-open space and feel the desire to explore or even run. Impulse control is not high on the list of strengths for children with autism, so you'll need to watch their wandering radius carefully. If your child will understand, give clear boundaries about how far is too far. You can stick a flag in the sand to give a visual indication of a boundary.

"When my family goes to the beach, we divide and conquer," says Sarah. "Jim is with my son all the time, period. And I stay with his brother and sister. It helps us both to know where to focus our energy and helps us all have a great time."

Snow Day!

Too far from the beach to surf waves? Perhaps you get enough snow in your area to surf on snow! Your child can get some of the same sensory benefits with these activities. Sledding will give your child a major sensory thrill and big action. Choose a hill that is not too steep and where other sliders have already packed the snow. Round disk sleds are easier to control than the traditional sled or toboggan, so use one of those if possible. Start with hills that will build confidence and save the major thrill rides for later, when you are both experienced sledders. Having certain hills in mind for "next year" can be a fun way to make oncoming winter more welcome.

When you are heading out for a snow adventure, pay particular attention to the sensory issues that will impact your spectrum child. Find that favorite pair of gloves, bring along an extra set of dry clothes, or have hot chocolate in a thermos to counteract a moment of despair. This kind of preparation will make your trip much more successful.

If your family likes to ski, check out your local resort's adaptive skiing options. Many places offer lessons for special needs kids that can make a big difference. Their equipment helps them teach kids with challenges the balance, stopping, and safety skills they'll need. If you are planning a ski trip, call ahead to the resort or slopes to find out if they offer these lessons. Instructors who have experience teaching special needs kids have a fund of patience and skill to draw from, and that will help you pick up where they leave off. Once your child has had a few lessons, joining you on the bunny slope may be more successful. Some ski resorts also hold great off-season programs and adaptive camps, so be sure to ask about those while you've got their attention.

Some questions to ask about a resort's adaptive skiing program:

- Are the lessons held on the main slopes, or is there an area away from the main resort?

- How long are the lessons, and what do they cost?

- How many instructors are there per child?

- Do they use any special equipment (like harnesses or a toboggan)?

- Will the instructor give parents some training so they can continue the learning process?

If you will be skiing with your child, make sure to take the necessary safety precautions. Judgment is a key aspect of skiing, especially when it is crowded. If this presents a problem for your child, you might want to borrow a harness (held by a skier behind the child on skis) to help guide them. Or consider starting your child with cross-country skiing before downhill or snowboarding. The experience of having skis on the feet may be easier for your child with practice on a flat course, and he can work up to the speed, confidence, and thrill of downhill skiing.

Ice skating is also a great way to learn to glide with something strapped on the feet, so if skiing is in your future, trips to the skating rink near your home will help develop the appropriate balance and sensory familiarity. The feeling of motion is also similar but can be better controlled, so the preparation will serve well.

Some other cold-weather tips:

- Do some experimentation between gloves and mittens. Some kids hate the feeling of individual fingers and want to be able to keep their digits together in a mitten. Once you figure out which is preferred, stock up!

- If your child won't tolerate either gloves or mittens, try layering a shirt that is a couple of sizes too big. The long sleeves will hang down over his hands and provide some protection. You can cut a hole for the thumb to poke through to increase its effectiveness.

- Always bring extra pairs of gloves or mittens. Wet gloves are inevitable and can become a big downer.

- If your child doesn't usually like hats, wait until you are outside in the cold to put one on. The feeling of relief and protection may outweigh his customary dislike.

- If knit caps continue to be seriously out of the question, try a baseball cap. The same hat that provides cover from the sun on hot days will contain body heat in the cold, and the consistency will help.

Getting on Wheels

Cycling is a popular family sport, but riding a bike may not come as easily to your child with autism as it does to other kids. There are so many elements to riding a bike, from coordinating movements of hands and feet, to using judgment in navigating, balancing, and braking. Some kids will have a hard time mastering it.

If riding is of interest to your child in the tricycle stage, be sure to capitalize on it heavily and encourage riding whenever possible. For young children, Kettler makes a tricycle with a parent push bar in the back. As kids get bigger, there are sturdy, large-sized tricycles available, but it is a good idea to move to a two-wheeler with training wheels as soon as you can.

The training wheels routinely installed by bike stores or that come built-in on discount store bikes can be less sturdy and designed for small children only. If your child with autism is graduating to a larger size bike, take the extra step of going to a quality bike shop and inquiring about sturdy, strong training wheels. The store can perform the installation and can hopefully keep the fee under $20. But keep in mind that these wheels will serve for much longer and be much safer than the plastic or cheap kind.

If your child is simply not yet showing interest in biking, or has low tone and finds it too difficult, look in thrift shops and among second-hand exercise equipment for a stationary bike that can be used by smaller people. Some are simply designed for adults with no room to downsize, but others will allow for significant lowering of the seat and pulling back the handlebars. A stationary bike can be great practice for the outdoor kind, removing the judgment piece and a large measure of the coordination elements, not to mention reducing the strength required. A child who masters the stationary bike will be in a stronger position to use a real bike soon.

There are programs such as Project Mobility that specialize in teaching kids with special needs to ride bikes. Keep an eye out for those or use the Internet to research a local option. Some programs use an intensive, weeklong approach of everyday lessons, adapted cycling equipment, and heavy supervision to get kids riding. But many of their techniques, especially their intensive approach, can be used by motivated parents. If you can find a school gymnasium that will allow you to work on biking indoors, you can minimize the danger of injury from falling off and eliminate the potential distractions of the outside world.

If your child has the physical capacity to ride a bike but lacks the judgment to ride on public streets, or he lacks the physical strength to propel the bike but really has the interest, consider a tandem bicycle. Ideally this two-person bike will be controlled from the rear.

The child rides in the front position so he can see and feel the wind on his face, but the steering and navigation is controlled by the adult in the back position. You can view tandem bikes at everykidmobility.com (the ATP 2600 Tandem), or the Buddy Bike (www.buddybike.com). Some companies offer financial assistance; if you are interested, explore it with them directly. Having this kind of bike can open up the world of cycling to the whole family. It means having a way for everyone to participate, planning picnics or longer rides together, and experiencing adventures not to be missed.

Sometimes local organizations offer adapted team sports for special needs kids. Check with other parents or parent organizations if you think your child would enjoy soccer, T-ball, or basketball. Often those programs are coached by parents of special needs kids themselves who can find ways to accommodate and include everyone. And the Special Olympics offers adapted sports programs for special needs kids throughout the year. Visit their website to find programs near you: www.specialolympics.org.

Give it a Sporting Chance

If your family has a hobby that you'd like to continue, don't give up. There are ways to adapt nearly anything, from sailing to camping to biking. It is important to be realistic about the expectations you place on everyone, but if there is something that means a lot to you, break it down. What is preventing you from pursuing it? How can that aspect be mitigated? Rather than walking away or pursuing it without your family, see if you can make it work.

Chapter 10

New Traditions and Holiday Celebrations

· · · · ·

Holidays can be a stressful time for everyone, and when you add autism to the mix, it becomes exponentially more complicated. Just enduring the holidays becomes the goal of many families. But it's time for us to set the bar higher than that! There are many ways to find joy and happiness during holidays with autism, but it requires creative thinking, planning ahead, and willingness to be unconventional. These are skills that parents of kids with autism hone every day. Sometimes family gatherings seem designed to be difficult for our kids to handle: large groups of people contained in smaller spaces, high levels of excitement, lots of talking, lots of excitement, lots of noise! Unfamiliar food, new faces, fancy clothes. Sparkly and fragile home decorations. Many change to usual routines, like late dinners, staying up past bedtime, and using guest bathrooms.

Be prepared to admit that there may be some gatherings or events that are simply not workable "as is" or within your power to change. When an event falls into that category, cut your losses and move on with something different. But you'll find that making the effort to change settings or events to meet your family's needs can pay dividends year after year.

Some Call it Love

Valentine's Day can be a socially intense holiday for kids. Fortunately most schools have caught on to the emotional trauma that selective-giving and popularity contests created in years of old. Most schools now decree more democratic versions of the holiday, especially in the elementary years. But usually an obligation remains for kids to produce paper Valentines for classmates, teachers, and aides, and it is a task that many kids with autism are supremely disinterested in for all its attention to penmanship, art, and social interaction. While creating valentines has undertones of therapeutic value (aside from the fine-motor aspects, it is a social holiday and the other kids will be participating), it can get old quickly.

You can help your child by simplifying the task as much as possible and adding interest anywhere you can. If you purchase commercial cards, look for some that use a character or movie your child enjoys. The idea of matching particular friends to the prewritten messages may sound fun at the outset, but be wary of adding this extra effort. It can make the whole process frustrating. For the more crafty or artistic, you can cut out hearts from construction paper and decorate with stickers, ink stamps, or cutouts.

Use your computer to print labels that say "Love, [your child's name]," which your child can apply instead of signing his name twenty-nine times. You can also make stickers with classmates' names so that your child can fly through that step too. Here's an example:

For these stickers, we used a template in Microsoft Word and inserted a snapshot. A standard printer will accept entire

sheets of these labels. For a custom touch, you can download decorative fonts at no charge by searching online.

The Bunny Hop

Since Easter always falls on a Sunday, it is a nice holiday to
explore with friends and family, leaving school issues out
of it. There are fun ways to have an Easter or springtime
celebration that will be fun for everyone.

Set up a multi-sensory egg hunt, hiding treat-filled
plastic eggs in varying degrees of difficulty. Always have
some that seem too easy to be believed. To really use the
sensory aspect to its fullest, have eggs operate in different
ways. Some can contain small noisemakers that chirp or
beep, for an auditory aspect. Others can contain lighted
superballs or other flashing toys so they sparkle and glow.
Keep the treats inside nonedible, because different diets
and allergies abound. Stickers are a great prize, as are small
plastic animals, beads, or marbles.

If church attendance is an important part of your life,
preparation will be the key to navigating the more important holidays. Find out in advance what activities your
church has planned for children. Are they going to be fun
for your child with autism, or overstimulating? Speak to
your pastor or the organizers about it. A church, temple, or

other place of worship is a great place to put your effort and energy. It will ultimately strengthen your relationship and enhance the ability of parishioners to relate to your family. Work with them to identify a quiet room where your child can retreat if things get to be too much; see if you can adapt art or food projects to be workable. Give people the information they need about your child's sensory issues and diet.

If you can establish a bank of projects and lessons that are accessible to your child, the church can keep them on hand for future events and other children as well. The time you spend assembling a cache will not only help your child but also other special needs children in the future. If your child has a home program or a well-established relationship with a therapist, you might find out if someone with expertise can spend some time consulting with your church about ways to adapt their programs. Sometimes talking to a professional will allow new people to raise concerns or correct misconceptions that they are shy about discussing with parents. And as always when you are pushing for more and better adaptability, offer to give your time and help them understand that their work will be important to everyone.

If Easter Sunday involves spending time at family parties, apply some of the same thinking you did with the church. Is there a quiet place that your child can retreat if the gathering becomes too loud? Would it be best to split up so that one parent can spend time with family while your child stays home with the other or does a separate activity?

Dividing the family on holidays is an especially difficult decision for parents. It is natural to want to include everyone in family gatherings and to devote significant efforts to making that a success. But some of these events can be very difficult for children on the spectrum. And when you remember the importance of considering the feelings of siblings too, all-or-some becomes a rough choice. Take it easy on yourself and resist carrying a lot of guilt about the way you eventually resolve the issue. We may envision our family enjoying a picture-perfect holiday, but we can't let that image blind us to reality.

While you want your extended family to remember, include, and love your special needs child, if large family gatherings are loud, crowded, and complicated, they may not be the best time to foster those relationships. If all of your time will be spent protecting other people's property and your child's fragile sense of control, splitting the family into separate groups and doing different things may be best. You'll need to consider if asking hostesses for accommodations and doing some additional preparation will help make the event work or if that will raise expectations and heighten stress. Make the decision that seems best, and don't beat yourself up if it turns out it wasn't the right choice. You'll learn from mistakes and find ways to make the next gathering even better.

Passover

The retelling of stories in a seder laden with symbolism and tradition involves some of a child's least favorite activities: sitting still, paying attention, and being quiet. But Passover is an important family time when participants recognize life's blessings amid hardship. In that spirit of love and endurance, call upon your family and friends for their contribution of patience, love, and creativity.

Try to set up an area where your child can play reasonably calmly, with toys that you won't have to oversee much. Set your own private goals for the ceremony: Are there particular parts that you'd like your child to be part of? Focus on what is within his ability and let him take breaks or even absent himself during the rest of the time if that is necessary. Perhaps asking the Four Questions is within reach, and they can be practiced in advance. They can also be reduced or truncated with the cooperation of your seder leader. Be sure to ask in advance to avoid surprises.

It can also help to have a colorful, child-friendly Haggadah, and there are short versions and a variety of styles available in bookstores and online. There is also a GF/CF Passover Guide available for those trying to combine kosher-for-Passover principles with this special diet (see Appendix for link).

The traditional game of hiding the afikomen can be revived if it has not been part of your family's seder for a while. This "hide the matzo" game is usually played toward the end of the meal, withheld as a way to keep all children patient and engaged! Be sure to explain the purpose of the game and the reward.

You can adapt the game by hiding several afikomen, each wrapped in a different colored napkin. Try to keep the napkins simple and easily differentiated, as opposed to plaids or busy prints that will become confusing. Depending on how many participants you have, assign each child or each group of kids a particular napkin color to find and explain that it is "against the rules" to tell other players where their napkin is hidden if it is spotted along the way. It may help to give the children an extra of "their" napkin to carry as they look. And the game may be more successful if you've been able to discuss it or practice in advance. Passover loans itself well to a Social Story. You can even show your child "his" napkin in the days prior to the event and practice finding it at home.

Consider also an abbreviated seder that can be expanded each year as your child becomes better able to understand and participate. Each year will bring you closer to the traditions you remember from your own childhood.

The Rockets' Red Glare

Independence Day happens during summer when your child may not be in school, so some of the learning that happens around other national holidays won't be built into this day. This is a great opportunity to take that over yourself, making it more fun, adding some excitement, and incorporating your child's interests as much as possible.

Check out the music and many games and books for kids with American content. *Schoolhouse Rock* has several video shorts about the simpler workings of government and the origins of the United States, and they are available on DVD, for download on iTunes, and even on YouTube. Check out their "No More Kings" for a short musical explanation of our nation's independence from England. Red, white, and blue art projects abound. You can also pick up some flags and pinwheels for your child. Flags and pinwheels in particular tend to appeal to children with autism because of their motion and sparkly flash. If your child is not hugely interested in art, try doing projects like decorating a finished pinwheel with silver ribbons or hanging flags around the house or yard.

It's a terrific holiday to spend outdoors since the weather is routinely clear and sunny in most parts of the country. Fly a red, white, and blue kite, and let your child hold the strings. Get out the pump rockets, or try some noisy poppers that can be flung at the ground. Fill water guns with super-cold water to provide an additional sensory surprise. Plan a barbeque or outdoor party, either in your own yard or at a nearby playground, so the kids have a structure to enjoy and a familiar environment amid a social time.

One great outdoor fun toy is as simple as a big bin of ice. Kids love to touch and play with ice, especially on a hot day. Try getting an extra bag of ice and dumping it into a plastic bin for kids to enjoy.

Fireworks shows are a major event in many communities. Don't rule it out immediately, but think carefully about whether your family should attend. There are a lot of factors to consider, such as your child's ability to handle loud and sudden noises, his usual bedtime (which may be much earlier than most fireworks shows), his overall interest in visual phenomena, and crowds that might be involved. Sometimes you can find a vantage point further away from the central audience location that will give you a less dramatic show but a much quicker getaway. Attending a fireworks show at the official viewing site will mean lots of traffic after the finale when everyone tries to leave at once. You may be able to better navigate these kinds of crowds with a special needs stroller.

"One of the best purchases we ever made," shares Ellen, "was our oversized stroller. Our son is not mobility impaired, but when it comes to crowds, he gets overwhelmed. We used to miss out on big stuff because we knew Dale wouldn't be able to manage getting there and holding his own in a crowd. But the stroller changed that; he can relax and let us do the 'driving.' If we know we will have to park our car far away or make our way through crowds, we throw it in the trunk. At our first fireworks show, there were huge crowds and a ridiculous parking situation. We took our time, parked a good distance away, and wheeled Dale and his little brother each in their own strollers. No problem! We enjoyed the show and both of them fell asleep on the walk back to the car. Now we take the stroller to amusement parks, airports, and other crowded places, and it has opened up a lot of doors for us!"

Some insurance plans will cover a portion of the cost of a special needs stroller (under the Durable Medical Equipment category). If having a large-sized stroller would help your family, it is worth investigating. Without supplementary funding they are costly, but you can see some options at Adaptivemall.com. Resist the urge to let embarrassment (he's too big for a stroller) or pride (he isn't handicapped!) stand in the way. There is no test of what a child's needs must be to use a special needs stroller. What matters is what works for your family! And staying home instead of using one just doesn't make sense.

The Spookiest Time of Year

Halloween can be a seasonal joy and a seasonal nightmare, in ways both intended and unintended. Anticipation and pressure tends to be very high at this time of year, so one of the most important tasks a parent has is keeping things in perspective.

Costumes can be a particular challenge for kids with autism because of the sensory factors involved. Masks, hats, and costume clothing all feel strange. Some kids may enjoy the idea of picking out a favorite character to imitate, but others will not see the point, and still other kids won't understand the holiday at all. But most parents try hard to find ways that our kids can participate. Halloween is a source of strong memories from our own childhoods, and it forms a central part of all social activity for that month.

For kids who are not interested or don't like the sensory feeling of costumes, here are some dress-up ideas that may get you through:

- *Soldier.* All it really needs is camouflage pants and an olive drab shirt from a discount store, and perhaps dog tags around the neck and a cap if it can be tolerated. Other accessories, like a clip-on compass or canvas belt, can be found at local military surplus stores if you want to take it further.

- *Sports figures.* The easiest and best go-to costume! All it requires is a big, comfy sports jersey and plain pants, but it can be embellished with headgear, shorts on top of pants for hockey players, tight pants for football players, sweatbands, or other signature touches. No problem to wear sneakers!

- *Motorcycle tough.* A black sleeveless t-shirt, a temporary tattoo, and a denim jacket or vest. Amp it up with leather-studded bracelet or black boots, or get creative by painting the back of the jacket with an image or using iron-on patches.

When it comes to trick-or-treating, most parents report that both age and repetition play important roles. Angela said, "The first two years we went trick-or-treating, Levi didn't understand. Why were people walking around at night? He looked at the lights, the decorations, but he didn't really get it. It was kind of sad for me. But we went around the neighborhood, and every few houses we knocked on the door and went through the routine. After a couple of years, the light bulb seemed to come on. He began to enjoy the trick-or-treating and take the initiative. He didn't really care about the candy, but the interaction was simple, predictable, and full of praise and fun. Since there was a time when I thought it wasn't possible for him to enjoy Halloween, I got almost as big a thrill out of his participation as he did!"

Jennifer found another route to victory: "My daughter was freaked out by Halloween, and all the excitement at school meant that by evening she was pretty anxious. So we suggested that she stay home and hand out candy to kids who came to the door instead of trick-or-treating. We role-played the routine a few times, and she got it down very quickly. Soon she really owned it! It has become 'her job' every Halloween and we've expanded into letting her choose the candy at the store and buy a new bowl every year. Seeing her have so much fun with it is the best."

Some kids understand and love Halloween right away, others need time to process the concepts and warm to it. Some may not ever understand or enjoy it. The issues that can crop up at school are myriad and not always predictable. If your child has some difficulty with the holiday, consider taking a "Personal Day" and going on a special outing instead, opting out of the parades and contests and creating your own special day. It is a good time to try a usually crowded venue that you have been avoiding, go to a morning matinee, or take a hike. If you end the day with a feeling of satisfaction, it doesn't matter whether you've done it the "traditional" way or not.

This is a key attitude to take through all holidays, especially as fall ramps up and the heavyweight holidays come fast and strong. It can begin to be a lot of pressure. The television bombards us, the stores assault us, and schools pull out their "themed" content in relentless style. Extended family traditions and overall expectations begin to mount, and the pressure can lead to tension around the house. Just know that kids feel it and react to it.

Giving Thanks

With its secular appeal and attention to food, Thanksgiving is a favorite holiday among many. But when food is problematic because of special diets or picky eating and family expectations rise, the elements of the holiday we love can feel like a conspiracy. One of the toughest parts of having a child with autism in the family is finding that pleasures you remember from childhood and looked forward to continuing can quietly go sour.

Take a deep breath and *prioritize.* If there are family gatherings that you simply must attend, think those through first. Do they involve travel? What will it be like for your kids? Will you end the experience with a feeling of connectedness and satisfaction, or is this an annual opportunity for torture? You can work through the event and adapt wherever possible. Or you can opt out. That's right, you can opt out. It may seem obligatory to go as a family to a relative's house some distance away. But if you find that you are annually stressed, frustrated, coping with an unhappy family, bickering with your spouse, and feeling attacked, take another look. Can you fulfill the obligation for a family visit at a less stressful time? Everything during the Thanksgiving and Christmas seasons is amplified—crowds, visual distractions, tempers. Visiting family for, say, a birthday, would involve much less difficulty.

Paul said, "Going to my mom's for Thanksgiving was such a regular tradition that it took us awhile to realize what a toll it was taking on our family. It is tough to travel at that time of year anyway, and long lines for extra security at the airport made it worse. We had a hard time maintaining a GF/CF diet in my mom's house, so Caleb tended to be even more hyper than usual because of lapses, which didn't help. Anna and I were totally exhausted by the end of the trip, and it felt like we were arguing about everything. Finally we had to admit that Thanksgiving needed a redesign. We couldn't keep it up."

Anna explains the aftermath. "At first we tried to invite the family to our house for Thanksgiving. Whoops, big mistake. We were not prepared for the reaction. Paul's mom got very hurt, telling us how hard she worked to make it a wonderful day and so on. We created such a ruckus that we split up into two groups that year, with

Paul taking our daughters to his mom's, and Caleb and me staying home. Talk about a bummer. But the following year we were more prepared. We went to see Paul's mom in August when the kids were off school, and we had a nice visit. On the last day we told her that we wouldn't be able to make it back for Thanksgiving. She accepted it with grace at that point. We were able to create a better tradition from then on, visiting Grandma in the summer and doing a cooperative Thanksgiving dinner at home with a few GF/CF friends."

Think about what you love or want to continue about any holiday and take that part forward. When it comes to Thanksgiving, family and food tend to be the focus. Some of the traditional food may need to be reconceived for dietary reasons or picky eating, so give the whole meal a long look. You don't need to keep making sweet potato casserole if no one wants to eat it, even if it was your favorite when you were a kid.

Sherry in Southern California shared her family's unconventional Thanksgiving: "When we stopped traveling to Seattle to be with my family on Thanksgiving, we started our favorite tradition of all: We bring turkey sandwiches and little pumpkin pies to the beach for a picnic!"

Here are other ideas from autism families:

- *Elaine in Portland says:* "We do a GF/CF Thanksgiving with friends who all have kids on the spectrum. But we have lunch instead of dinner, so when we've all had a great meal, we can head to the park for some swing time."

- *Diana in New York:* "We go to a Thanksgiving meal held by our church. All the kids have plenty of places to play in the classrooms, and my son is used to it. The grown-ups make a cooperative meal, and everyone brings a favorite."

- *Abby in Austin:* "I discovered the already prepared Thanksgiving dinner at Whole Foods, and it saved our holiday. I don't work in the kitchen all day anymore. Last year we went on a bike ride in the afternoon and then had my sisters' families over for dinner. It is easier for Jake to be at home. We have a great time!"

Everyone wants to create a holiday that their kids can look back on fondly. Traditions are great when they work. But don't be afraid to reexamine them when they don't. If an approaching holiday inspires dread, reconsider!

Christmas Cheer

Christmas can be like Thanksgiving in terms of family and church obligations, but often it is more intense. Reapply the same standard here of looking at what you consider "obligatory" and making difficult choices if you must. If you've got a child with autism, the need to make difficult choices is probably not a new concept. But it is easy to forget that holidays are a matter of choice. If you decide to travel for family gatherings, make your plans with short fuses in mind.

Bill recounts, "We were in the Midwest visiting my family over Christmas. There were lots of family parties, and we got together for meals, outings, entertainment, church, and so on. By the end of Day Two, it was clear that our son Jonah was maxed out. He couldn't handle the whole scene. Excited voices, crowded rooms, unfamiliar surroundings, new people, and expectations. We were staying with my mom, so there was no time that was just our family. So on Day Three, we booked the smallest, cheapest hotel room we could find. We didn't sleep there, but we used it as a retreat. Jonah watched TV, flopped on the bed, took a long bath, and just played away from everyone else. It really worked for him. And his sister Kyra played well with her cousins. Jonah was able to handle the gatherings we brought him to after that because he'd had quiet time. From now on we'll have some amount of private time every day when we travel. We saw what a huge difference it makes."

It isn't necessary to rent a hotel room, although it is a good option if you can. If you are among family, perhaps you can go to one relative's house while everyone else is gathering at another place. Even driving around in a rented car can be a nice getaway from all the excitement and noise. Finding some non-public time can be critical to making the holiday go smoothly.

Eight Crazy Nights

Hannukah gives kids with autism an extended opportunity to absorb and anticipate their participation, with the repetition of eight nights of short blessings and candle lighting, the retelling of the story of Hannukah, and all the great games to be played.

There are many ways for kids to participate in the holiday, including through gift giving. One method that seems to work well and distribute the responsibility is to assign each night of Hannukah to a different member of the family. One night Grandma and Grandpa might give gifts to everyone; another night it might be a sister or parent. This means that there will be at least one night of Hannukah where each participant is a giver but not a receiver. It helps to underscore the feelings associated with both roles. And when your child has his night to give, he can focus on interactions with each member of the family one at a time.

As your child gets older, allow him to help light candles. Taking appropriate precautions against accidental dropping or wax dripping is well worth the true feeling of participation it will create for your child to have a "lighting night" as well as a giving night.

Once is Almost Never Enough

Birthdays are fun but sometimes tricky. Finding the right mix of celebration without going overboard on pressure is a balancing act, and the threshold is different for every child. Family birthday celebrations should always be focused on what is actually fun for your particular family and not necessarily what is thought of as traditionally fun and "to be expected." If your child doesn't like cake but loves chocolate chip cookies, make a substitution. If parties with lots of kids are not something he'll enjoy, don't force it. Just keep the celebration to the few who will be sure to create a feeling of enjoyment.

Here are some ideas for fun family birthday traditions:

- Record on video the part of the day where you sing happy birthday to your child. Be sure to say or sing his new age. Burn it to CD or put it on the computer where he can have access to it easily. He'll enjoy it long after the day is over!

- If you are planning a party, be sure to center it around an activity that your child really enjoys. That will take pressure off the need to interact with lots of people because all the kids will get engaged in the activity.

- In the week leading up to your child's birthday, look at photos from previous year's celebrations, read books about birthdays together, and watch videos that have birthday themes. These will help build anticipation, which is half the fun of birthdays. Search Amazon for "birthday" to get book and video ideas.

- Use one number-shaped candle on your cake or treat instead of multiple single candles. It will help to reinforce the new age number visually as well as reduce the blowing power required.

- Familiar and beloved characters are often used on piñatas as well as on plates and decorations. If your child has a favorite, be sure to use it to increase interest. If he doesn't have a favorite or you can't find what you hoped, check out the decorations and piñatas in the shape of your child's new age.

- Develop your own party games based on your child's interest or favorite character. Have a Dora the Explorer Treasure Hunt in the backyard, invite kids to bring their own tracks to a Thomas the Tank Engine party, or hold a Lego building party. Always focus on the wonderful effort that everyone made rather than picking one "winner."

The most important thing about holidays and special events is to look down the long road. Even if a particular celebration is not a terrific success one year, experiencing it and helping everyone do their best is what becomes important. "Once and done" is not our way. Each year, your strategies and stresses make the holiday better for next year. It may take a few times for events to really sink in and for everyone to understand the expectations involved. But understanding will come for everyone who participates. With each successive year, the time will become more fun and enriching. Each year is an opportunity to repeat and relearn the lessons. Along the way, children will shift from relearning each and every time into anticipating what they remember. That shift will make all your efforts worthwhile.

Chapter 11

If You're Going to Dream, Dream Big!

· · · · · ·

Here are some big-ticket adventures that a family can dream about, save up for, or if you are lucky, go ahead and try! If you live near one of these places, so much the better. If you're farther away, it is an adventure in the making.

Vacations are sometimes written off as a "thing of the past" by parents with young children, especially if they have special needs. But they don't have to be. A trip is a wonderful way to develop closer family bonds and shared memories to last a lifetime. Teaching your kids to adjust to new environments is also an important life skill. And finally, having something big and fun on your calendar is one of the most wonderful ways to cope with day-to-day stress. Somehow, just knowing that an exciting and fun event is in the works can color everything you do with a hint of anticipation. Go ahead, plan a vacation! It can be as close as a two-day road trip to an amusement park or as ambitious as a flight to somewhere far away. But you'll never know if you don't try. Our kids sometimes surprise us by rising to new occasions. Here are some ideas that would really be worth the effort.

Zorbing

Zorbing is an activity you might have to see to believe, so perform a search on that term on YouTube to check out some videos of the thrill in action. What you'll find are videos of huge, clear, inflated spheres with an inner sphere in the center. They are large enough for two people to strap inside, and once secure, the entire ball is hurtled headlong down a huge hill. Am I kidding? No! If you have a child on the spectrum who loves adventure, craves motion, and is thrilled by novelty, this is a dream for you.

The Zorb is an adventure that hails from a creative bunch in New Zealand, and it is still most easily found there. The first United States-based site, Zorb Smokey Mountains, recently opened in Tennessee. Visit Zorb.

com to plan your vacation and adventure if this one appeals to you.

Downhill Thrills

Two great things that go great together—swimming and hurtling downhill! Have you and your family tried water-sliding? There may be indoor and outdoor water slides in your home area. And if your child enjoys these and might be ready for an even bigger thrill, consider a trip to Mason, Ohio to visit The Beach Waterpark. They have white sand, tropical palm trees, and most importantly, one of the most thrilling water slides in existence.

And while you are adventure seeking in Ohio, be sure to visit the Cedar Point Amusement park, which boasts one of the most thrilling roller coasters in the entire world, "The Dragster."

Cedar Point is a great destination for a wide variety of thrill rides and water sports. You can learn more about them at their website (www.cedarpoint.com). In addition to water slides, water rides, roller coasters, and carousels, they offer Jet Skis and parasailing too. Younger Jet Skiers and parasailers (under 100 pounds) can be accompanied by an adult.

As with many amusement parks, Cedar Point does have a special needs pass for families of children who have autism. At Cedar Point, the pass is good for parties of four, and it allows people to ride any ride the first time without waiting in line. Repeat rides require waiting in the same line as all other riders. Stop at the Customer Service Booth on your way into the park to request a pass.

Extreme Sports

Are you and your family into Extreme Sports? You might want to check out the Extreme Sports Camp in Aspen, Colorado. They are an individualized camp that creates outdoor sports programs in the Roaring Fork Valley of Colorado for kids and young adults with autism. They have a 1:1 camper-to-counselor ratio, and they take fifteen campers per session. They teach kids to climb on indoor walls, challenge ropes course, and outdoor cliffs with rappelling, rock hopping, and Tyrolean lines; water sports like skiing, tubing, wakeboarding, and boat surfing; and whitewater kayaking and rafting. They also go hiking, mountain biking, and swim in pools with giant water slides. Ready to sign up? Visit their website at Extremesportscamp.org.

Island Getaways

Pebbles Resort in Jamaica boasts not only the crystal clear waters, white sand beaches, warm sun, and coral reefs you think of when you imagine a trip to Jamaica but also a "vacation nanny." Folks say that when you've tried it, you'll never travel any other way. When you book your stay, the cost of an eight-hour-a-day helper is part of the total fee, and additional hours can be added for a nominal cost ($4 per hour). They have lots of special needs families come, so they have good expertise on their staff, and what's more, they sometimes offer incredible deals on their website, discounting as much as 50 percent off their package rates for families with special needs kids. Unlike other all-inclusive resorts where they tend to offer group activities that are led by a pool of staff and caregivers, Pebbles gives families the opportunity to get to know and develop a rhythm with their own vacation nanny, and that kind of familiarity can be essential to the comfort of some kids. (Visit their website at http://fdrholidays.com)

Is cruising for you? Some cruise lines are offering trips specifically for families of children with autism. Before taking a cruise, it would be a good idea to test the waters by going on a shorter boat ride. Even though cruise ships are extremely large and much more stable than a small craft, there is still the feeling of motion underfoot. Many families report that this suits their child perfectly, and the contained nature of the boat and ability to plan entertainment carefully is a great benefit. If this sounds like a vacation your family would love, visit Autism on the Seas to learn more (www.alumnicruises.orgAutism/Autism_Home.htm).

See the World

If your child fits into the category of "high-functioning young adult," you might like to check out Frontier Travel Camp. They arrange tours for groups and work on social skills and flexibility in an exciting and adventurous way, with staff that understands the needs of their clients and plans destinations with specifics in mind. Everything from the food to the method of travel is considered carefully, and the staff is experienced.

They book trips throughout the United States and Canada, including Hawaii and Alaska. They've also made trips to Europe (Italy, England, Scotland, Scandinavia, Russia, and the Baltics). To learn more, visit their website at www.frontiertravelcamp.com.

Family Camp

There are a variety of family camps all over the United States that allow families to stick together so parents can oversee their kids' needs even while having a fun getaway from the routines of home. These camps tend to be reasonably priced and offer our kids a combination of familiarity (Mom and Dad) and away-from-home adventure, which is more manageable than either a public vacation or a sleep-away camp on their own. Finding a camp that works for your family will pay dividends by providing escape and adventure year after year.

If you use the Advanced Search feature at the American Camp Association (www.campparents.org), you can look for both "autism" (under Special Needs) and "family sessions" to find a possibility near you. One of the biggest challenges about taking vacations away from home can be the unfamiliarity of new sleeping arrangements, so be sure to investigate the accommodations and think about whether it will work for your crew. Camps can offer a wide range of possibilities, from tents to large or small cabins, some with electricity, some without. Most family camps happen in summertime, but there are some year-round options.

A truly special camp is the Earthshine Mountain Lodge in North Carolina. They have an 80-foot-high, two-hour zip line course that will knock your socks off as it runs through trees in a heady, high-off-the-ground ride. They have an unplug-the-technology approach, which may sound a bit intimidating if your child is a screen junkie, but there is so much to do that you might find the break a great way to reduce the screen time when you get back home. Visit www.earthshinelodge.com

Other Zip Line Tours

You can find other amazing zip line adventures around the United States and beyond by searching www.adventure drop.com/AdventureTypes-Zip-Lines.html. Safety is key, and riders wear a strong harness and are sturdily strapped in before they go. But always call the facility before you arrive and talk to them about your child's height and weight, as well as his autism. Make sure everyone is comfortable before showing up. For a big adventure, there are zip line adventures (also known as canopy tours) in Costa Rica and Mexico, offering a unique, up-high perspective on the rain forests below. There are also U.S.-based tours, such as Redwood Canopy Tours in Mount Hermon, California. Learn more at http://mounthermon.org/redwood-canopy-tours.

Dune Buggying

Ever dreamed about rocking a dune buggy? It has elements of fun that our kids love, like fast moves, beaches, and family time. You can rent a dune buggy in a variety of cities, from those located along the Oregon Coast to others in Arizona, Florida, and California. If you Google "dune buggy rental," you'll be able to look through a variety of options. Add your location to see if any are available near you. An adult will have to do the driving at all times. But kids will have an amazing adventure strapped into the passenger seat. Some places have dune buggies that seat up to five or smaller ones that are just two-seaters. With a picnic packed in the back, you'll have a sand adventure that you'll never forget!

Houseboating or Yachting Family-Style

If you've got a child who loves the feeling of rhythmic rocking in a boat but is not as interested in crowds and public spaces, a house boating vacation might be the perfect getaway for you. In addition to that constant feeling of movement, you'll have a familiar place to sleep every night, kitchen facilities, and in some cases, a hot tub right on board. Nights are peaceful and serene, days present lake recreation opportunities galore, like Jet Skis, swimming, and water skiing. In fact, the rates for a houseboat that sleeps ten are less expensive than what you'd pay for hotel rooms or a house rental for the same sleeping capacity. And what an adventure!

The Ultimate Trampoline Experience

If your family likes jumping on a home trampoline, this next adventure is for you. In several locations around California, Sky High Sports offers a unique experience that you may have to see to believe. Visit their website at www. jumpskyhigh.com to take a look at their facility, which boasts trampolines as far as the eye can see—on the floor, on the walls, and everywhere you can imagine! Families can jump and jump and jump—there is no end to the creativity of the game playing, sports explosion, and gravity-defying heights that can be reached. But be warned: This is about the best exercise imaginable. You'll feel the motion and the burn! Your child may never want to leave.

BodyFlying

Another new sport springing up in some locations is that of indoor skydiving in a vertical wind tunnel. If you've ever dreamed of jumping out of airplanes or wondered if your child would like the free-fall sensation, you can find out with minimal risk by giving this a try.

iFly (http://iflysfbay.com) in particular welcomes families with special needs kids, and they make sure their first-time flyers feel safe and have fun. They have huge fans that generate the same windspeed that jumpers would feel when they fall. You start only a foot or two off the ground and are well-protected in safety gear and goggles. You're also within reach of an experienced instructor at all times. They welcome flyers over age three, and they are excited to make everyone feel safe but also feel like they're flying!

Dreaming Both Big and Small

The best dreams of all are the ones that have a hope of becoming real. Adventure is truly where you find it. If there is something you'd like to try that seems out of reach, get creative and take your family as close to the feeling as you can.

There is exciting fun in your neighborhood, not just on warm Caribbean beaches. Having a child with autism is a challenge, no question, but don't lose sight of the joy that life holds for those who are open to it. Autism does not have to become the central fact about your family. It is sure to be part of the picture. And autism changes the way you approach both everyday life and opportunity for adventure. Just don't let it stop you from experiencing adventure at all.

We all get just one life. Live yours and show your children that you can taste what the world has to offer—no matter your challenges.

Appendix

· · · · ·

Handicapped Placard

http://arthritis.about.com/od/driving/a/handicapparking.
htm

Places to Find Fun

Pump it Up—www.pumpitupparty.com
Sky High Sports—www.jumpskyhigh.com
iFly—www.iflysfbay.com
Sensory Friendly Films—www.autism-society.org/site/
PageServer?pagename=sensoryfilms

Swings and Things

All of these sites carry different sensory equipment and swings.

IKEA—www.ikea.com/us/en/catalog/categories/departments/childrens_ikea

Southpaw—www.southpawenterprises.com

TFH Special Needs Toys—www.specialneedstoys.com

Therapro—www.therapro.com

One Stop Sensory Shop—www.onestopsensoryshop.com

Hammocks.com—www.hammocks.com

Weighted Blankets—You can often find good prices on weighted blankets by looking on eBay for a supplier instead of going through a specialty therapy supply house.

Great Tools

Flip Video Camera—www.theflip.com—For capturing and sharing your adventures as well as preparing your child for new destinations with some advance reconnaissance. These video cameras take good quality video and plug right into a computer's USB port, making download and conversion effortless. Find them at your local electronics store or buy online.

iPod touch—www.apple.com/ipodtouch

iPad—www.apple.com/ipad

These are terrific fun for kids and adults alike, as well as offering a strong array of practical tools for locating, communicating, and mapping. Use it to play games, look up something in the yellow pages, find a nearby playground, listen to music, watch a video on YouTube, search on Google, or map a new destination. Record voice memos and convert to text for editing and email. Download a dictionary or find new gluten free recipes. The possibilities are endless!

OtterBox—www.otterbox.com—Don't leave your iPod, iPad, or iPhone unprotected in the hands of a child who may not understand how to take care of it. OtterBoxes are terrific crashproof cases that protect the investment. They also sell waterproof cases, which make it possible to listen to music just about anywhere.

Carabiners (REI)—www.rei.com/category/4500079—These have tons of practical uses, but most importantly can be used to hang a swing. Put one at the top of your swing hook to make it easy to switch to a different swing in just a moment. Your child will love the variety, and you'll enjoy the ease of use. Always verify the weight-bearing load it can handle.

Vista Print—www.vistaprint.com—You can get free business cards here, which are great tools for communicating with other parents you meet or for strangers who might need a quick education on why your child's behavior is unusual in public.

Getting Dressed

Shoes

Zappos—www.zappos.com—They have a huge variety of kids' shoes and a good search engine. Try looking there for shoes with Velcro closures by searching under "hook and loop."
WePlay Sports—www.weplaysports.com/wrestling/shoes— For those hard-to-find high-tops with Velcro closures, wrestling sneakers are the answer!
Vans—www.Vans.com—For Velcro and pull-on-style sneakers and supercool T-shirts that evoke skateboarding and surfing.

Clothing

Land's End—www.landsend.com—For pants with elastic waist in slim and husky sizes, and everything in between.
Swim Outlet—www.swimoutlet.com—For rash guards, swim trunks, goggles, and more.

Tools

Stitch Witchery—www.amazon.com/Dritz-Stitch-Witchery-Regular-Tape/dp/B0001DSIHI

Identification

Iron-on Labels—www.irononcamplabels.com
Temporary tattoos—http://straytats.com

Medical IDs and Temporary tattoos—Petite Baubles
Boutique—www.petitebaublesboutique.com

T-shirts

Shirt Crazy Kids World—www.kidsonlyworld.com
Shirts 4 Squirts—www.shirts4squirts.com
Website for your child's favorite TV program, such as
www.Nickjr.com
Disney—www.disneystore.com
Zazzle.com—www.zazzle.com/kids#kids

Connecting with Other Parents

Yahoo Groups—http://groups.yahoo.com
Google Groups—http://groups.google.com

Perform a search on "autism" and your location for the most targeted group possible. Sometimes there are also groups for specific interests like biomedical intervention, insurance reimbursement, and behavioral therapy. Start by finding a general group in your area and add from there.

Some groups are listed publicly and will come back from a search easily. Others are kept private and not listed in the main search directory. Ask local parents what groups they like best to discover any that might be operating without a public listing. Craigslist—www.craigslist.org

You can use your local Craigslist to find everything from used sporting goods and equipment to materials and toys for therapy. Start at the top level for your area and delve down in the free forums for your community. If you are looking for something in particular, you can post yourself without having to reveal your email address.

Party and Holiday Supplies, Teaching Tools

Oriental Trading—www.orientaltrading.com
Look for party supplies with favorite characters, and also check their Teaching Supplies section (particularly under "Teaching Supplies," then "Movement and Dance") for fun and inexpensive tools to use in fun and home programs. Also a great place to find small toys for Easter egg hunts, Mardi Gras beads, and much more.
Lakeshore Learning—www.lakeshorelearning.com
Another great site for supplies and teaching tools.

Passover

30 Minute Seder—www.30minuteseder.com
The Santa Cruz Haggadah: Kids Edition—www.amazon. com/Santa-Cruz-Haggadah-Kids/dp/0962891304

GF/CF Passover Guide—www.gfcfpassoverguide.com

Organizations

Ride a Wave Foundation—www.rideawave.org

Heart of Sailing—www.heartofsailing.org

Best Day Foundation—www.bestdayfoundation.org

Special Olympics—www.specialolympics.org

Finding a Camp

American Camp Association—http://find.acacamps.org/finding_special_needs.php

My Summer Camps.com—www.mysummercamps.com/camps/Special_Needs_Camps/

Therapy/Respite Camps for Kids—http://wmoore.net/therapy.html

Kids Camps.com—www.kidscamps.com/specialneeds camps.camp

Dreaming Big

Extreme Sports Camp—www.extremesportscamp.org

Zorbing—www.zorb.com

The Beach Waterpark—http://thebeachwaterpark.com

Cedar Point—www.cedarpoint.com

Pebbles Resort, Jamaica—http://fdrholidays.com

Autism on the Seas—www.alumnicruises.orgAutism/Autism_Home.htm

Frontier Travel Camp—www.frontiertravelcamp.com

Earthshine Mountain Lodge—www.earthshinelodge.com

Adventure Drop—www.adventuredrop.com
AdventureTypes-Zip-Lines.html

Redwood Canopy Tours—http://mounthermon.org/redwood-canopy-tours

Houseboating.org—www.houseboating.org

Sky High Sports—www.jumpskyhigh.com

iFly—http://iflysfbay.com

Entertainment Websites for Kids

Starfall—www.starfall.com

PBS Kids—http://pbskids.org

Nick Jr.—www.nickjr.com

Totlol—www.totlol.com

YouTube—www.youtube.com